Learning Disability - An Overview

By

Dr. Deepti Tewari

Ira Publishers

Kanpur, Uttar Pradesh

ISBN : 978-93-93705-28-0
Fist Edition : 2023
LEARNING DISABILITY - AN OVERVIEW by DR. DEEPTI TEWARI
Cover Page : Google | Composing : Printlok

Ira Publishers
405 B, C, Navsheel Jyoti Apartment
127/219-A, Juhi Kalan, Kidwai Nagar,
Kanpur Nagar-208014, U.P., India
e-mail : irapublishers@gmail.com
www.iraimaginations.com
www.facebook.com/irapublisher.in

Abstract

A learning disability presents itself on a functional and behavioural level as slow or abnormal learning of new skills. Among school-aged children, these difficulties may be seen as deficient skills in reading, spelling and writing, reading comprehension, mathematics, problem-solving and attention. These deficits in cognitive functions prevent the child from achieving the learning objectives parallel to age group in spite of sufficient schooling and teaching.

Accordingto a study conducted among children in US,learning disability affects up to 10%of school children. In a review of Indian studies on prevalence of learning disability, prevalence of various types of deficits of scholastic skills was reported to be 3-10% among the student population. In this review, studies had screened students for dyscalculia, dyslexia and different type of learning disabilities in the States of Karnataka, Kerala and Tamil Nadu. In another study from rural India, prevalence of specific learning disability was reported to be 13% in primary school children.

But at present, in India, the concept of Dyslexia is limited to few big cities only. Even the doctors and top professional in education system are unaware about the exact nature of the disability and the methods for its remediation. The school teachers are not trained to identify these learning disabilities and there is a scarcity of professionals trained to diagnose dyslexia and provide proper interventions. Parents of suffering children generally have no clue how to deal with the situation and majority of them keep punishing the child for poor performance, which in turn results in development of severe behavioural and personality problems in the child.

The present work is a compilation of information about various aspects of learning disability with an aim to provide its readers basic information about the disability.

It describes the various types of learning disabilities i.e. dyslexia, dysgraphia, dyscalculia, auditory processing disorder, language processing disorder, non-verbal learning disabilities and visual perceptual deficit. It also emphasizes the fact that the various types of learning disabilities are not individual entities, they occur as an spectrum and the symptoms overlap so that no two children have exactly same problem.

It also gives a basic understanding about the process of learning and the causation of the learning disabilities. This understanding will help the readers to work out their own intervention methods while dealing with children having learning disabilities. In addition, some typical ways to handle specific problems are also mentioned.

The book also mentions the probable outcomes that are seen in children with learning disabilities along with a chapter on the ways by which these children can be supported for a better outcome.

The chapter on parenting describes the problems faced by the parents of the children having learning disability along with few parenting tips. The aim is to make people understand the trauma and the challenges faced by the parents and the family. It is also aimed at creating an acceptance of the overall situation among the parents by accepting their own emotional responses and struggles.

The book also describes the emotional status of the suffering children and their struggles in order to create and empathy for these children among the society. The last chapter describes few cases so that people get a real life picture of the problem and are able to identify the problem in any child around them. The list of successful people having learning disabilities is compiled with an aim to provide a positive outlook towards the problem.

Overall, the work is aimed at providing a basic information about learning disabilities in simple words in order to make people aware about the various aspects of the condition.

Contents

CHAPTER 1
Introduction

Thomas Edison was born in Ohio in 1847. When he was seven, his family moved to Michigan where he spent most of his childhood. He was a poor student and could not learn by the usual teaching ways by which other children learnt. In 1854, Reverend G.B.Engle, Thomas's school headmaster belittled him by calling him "addled". This outraged the youngster and he stormed out of the school. His mother Nancy, a teacher by profession, brought him back to school next day to discuss the situation with Reverend Engle, but she became angry at his rigid ways. Everything was forced on the kids. She withdrew her son from the school where he had been for only three months and resolved to educate him at home. Although he seems to have briefly attended two more schools, nearly all his childhood learning took place at home.

This is the story of childhood of Thomas Elva Edison who later on proved to be a genius and became a brilliant scientist and inventor. There are many other well-known people who could not do well at school levels and struggled with their basic education. Some of these include scientist Albert Einstein, physicist and astronomer Galileo Galilei, actor Tom Cruise, filmmaker Steven Spielberg, designer Tommy Hilfiger, boxer Mohammad Ali, businessman Steve Jobs and so on.

All of the above mentioned people were/are suffering from learning disability.

The term learning disability refers to a broad range of disorders that impair an individual's academic and functional abilities. These abilities are generally those of speaking, listening, reading, writing, spelling, reasoning and the ability to organize information. Due to impairment of these abilities, at a first glance, the child appears as if he has intellectual impairment. However, a learning disability is by no means an indicator of lower intelligence levels. In fact, to the very contrary, research has shown that individuals with learning disabilities may actually have normal or even above normal intelligence levels.

Learning disability is a fairly recent diagnosis. Researchers studied the psychological disabilities for long before arriving upon the term "learning disability". It also brought to light the many individuals in the past who had exhibited symptoms of one learning disability or the other. During their own lifetimes, however, they were neither diagnosed nor properly treated for their disabilities and their condition kept confusing themselves as well as those around them.

CHAPTER 2
History of Learning Disabilities

During 1800s till mid-1900s, people in general were unaware of learning and attention issues. Those affected by these conditions were generally sidelined from the normal education system. However, the doctors and scientists had started recognizing and acknowledging these problems. In 1877, German neurologist Adolf Kussamaul coined the term "word blindness" to describe "complete text blindness…although the power of sight, the intellect and the powers of speech are intact". In 1887, German physician Rudolf Berlin used the term "dyslexia" for the first time to describe "very great difficulty in interpreting written or printed symbols". In 1895, Ophthalmologist James Hinshelwood described the case of acquired word blindness in medical journal "The Lancet" where a 58 year old man awoke one morning to discover that he could no longer read. Hinshelwood continued to study word blindness in children, and recognized the need for early identification of these children by teachers. After reading Dr. Hinshelwood's report, Dr. W. Pringle Morgan, in 1896, wrote in the "British Medical Journal" about a 14 year old boy who seemed to have word blindness from birth. He was described as bright, intelligent and quick, but had great difficulty reading and spelling despite the efforts of his teachers. Morgan wrote: "The schoolmaster who has taught him for some years says that he would be the smartest lad in the school if the instruction were entirely oral". And then, in 1905, the first report of childhood reading difficulties was published by ophthalmologist Dr. W.E. Burner in U.S. and finally, it was in 1963 that Samuel A. Kirk used the term "learning disability" for the first time in a conference in Chicago. By this time, the problem had attention of a large number of people at all levels and events started happening in quick succession.

In 1964, Association of Children with Learning Disabilities (ACLD) was created in U.S. This association is now known as Learning Disabilities Association of America (LDA) and it has chapters in every state.

In 1968, ADHD first appeared in Diagnostic and Statistical Manual (DSM) by the name of "hyperkinetic impulse disorder".

It was in 1969 that the U.S. Congress passed the first federal law mandating support services for children with learning disabilities. This was called Children with Specific Learning Disabilities Act. Further laws were made in 1973 and 1975 which prohibited discrimination against people with disabilities and ensured free appropriate public education for all children.

In 1977, Pete and Carrie Rozelle founded the National Centre for Learning Disabilities. Being parents of a child with LD, their aim was to help and support other families having children with learning disability.

During 1980s and 1990s till now, more and more research work is being done to find out the exact cause of these problems. Simultaneously, the condition has gained more acceptance and people have become more aware of the existence of such problems. The sufferers and their parents are being given more and more rights to ensure that these children are able to lead a normal productive life.

However, in developing countries like India, the awareness and acceptance level of these problems is still very less. Even the people in education and health sectors are not aware of the nature of these problems. The Indian government has passed certain rules and has given some additional facilities to ensure education for such children but the children and their parents are either unaware of their rights or are struggling to actually get those facilities at school level. Apart from this, there is a severe deficiency of qualified persons to deal with such problems. As a result, the children suffering from learning disabilities are generally sidelined and remain deprived of proper school education except in certain bigger cities.

CHAPTER 3
What is Learning Disability?

Generally speaking, learning disability is a neurological disorder. In simple terms, a learning disability results from a difference in the way a person's brain is "wired." Generally, children with learning disabilities are as smart, or even smarter than their peers. But they may have difficulty reading, writing, spelling, reasoning, recalling and/or organizing information if left to figure things out by themselves or if taught in conventional ways. A learning disability can't be cured or fixed; it is a lifelong issue. With the right support and intervention, however, children with learning disabilities can succeed in school and go on to successful, often distinguished careers later in life.

3.1 Definition

As per the U.K. Department of Health, a learning disability is defined as a significantly reduced ability to understand new or complex information, to learn new skills (impaired intelligence), with a reduced ability to cope independently (impaired social functioning), which started before adulthood".

As per the American body 'National Joint Committee for Learning Disability', "learning disability is a generic term that refers to a heterogeneous group of disorders manifested by significant difficulties in the acquisition and use of listening, speaking, reading, writing, reasoning or mathematical abilities. These disorders are intrinsic to the individual and are presumed to be due to central nervous system dysfunction. Even though a learning disability may occur concomitantly with other handicapping conditions (e.g. sensory impairment, mental retardation, social and emotional disturbance etc.) or environmental influences (e.g. cultural differences, insufficient/ inappropriate instruction, psychogenic factors etc.), it is not the direct result of these conditions or influences".

Using the word "generic term" means learning disabilities is a global term under which a variety of specific disorders can be reasonably grouped.

The second critical element of the definition is "heterogenous group of disorders" which means that the disorders grouped under the learning disability label are specific and different in their nature. This also implies that the specific causes of the disorders are also many and dissimilar.

The third element of the definition is "manifested by significant difficulties" which implies that the presence of learning disabilities handicaps and seriously limits the performance of some of the key abilities in the affected person. This element was specially included in the definition to emphasize the fact that the presence of learning disabilities in an individual can be as debilitating as the presence of cerebral palsy, mental retardation, blindness or any other handicapping condition.

The next key element of the definition "in the acquisition and use of listening, speaking, reading, writing, reasoning or mathematical abilities" means that to be considered learning disabled, an individual's disorder must result in serious impairment of one or more of the above listed abilities.

The next phrase is "intrinsic to the individual". This means that the source of the disorder is found within the person who is affected. The disability is not imposed on the individual as a consequence of economic deprivation, poor child-rearing practices, faulty school instruction, societal pressures, cultural differences etc. Where present, such factors may complicate the treatment, but they are not considered to be the cause of the learning disability.

And the last key component of the definition is "presumed to be due to the central nervous system dysfunction." This signifies that the cause of the learning disability is a known or presumed dysfunction in the central nervous system. Such dysfunctions may be by-products of traumatic damage to tissues, inherited factors, biochemical insufficiencies or imbalances or other similar conditions that affect the central nervous system.

3.2 Symptoms of Learning Disability

As discussed earlier, LD is a global neurological disorder affecting a wide range of functions of the individual. The result is emergence of academic problems. Inability to perform well in school is the one central problem which every child with LD faces and in most of the cases, this is the first thing which attracts the attention of parents towards presence of a neurological deficit in their child. The reason for not being able to cope in school may vary from child to child. The child may have a trouble in reading, writing or working with numbers. He or she can also have a problem in expressing himself or herself verbally and/

or by writing. They may have a problem in organizing their thoughts so that they are constantly confused. They can also have problem in sitting still and paying attention during classes or they can have a problem in adjusting in social groups and situations so that they remain in constant anxiety and are unable to concentrate on studies.

Every child who has LD has one or more of the following problems which together lead to a poor academic performance which is incongruent to their intelligence levels.

1. Attention problems – A child with LD may have one or more of the following :

- Is easily distracted
- Cannot pay attention to minute details
- Cannot handle multiple tasks simultaneously
- Has problems in following instructions
- Has poor impulse control so that he or she acts and/or speaks without thinking
- Is hyperactive
- Remains lost and it appears as if the child is day-dreaming
- Lacks patience
- Is restless and remains anxious

2. Problems in communication skills – These include :

- Trouble with written or spoken language
- Trouble with getting thoughts on paper
- Poor grammar
- Poor spelling skills
- Problems with copying information from book or blackboard

- Writing slowly
- Poor handwriting
- Poor understanding of spoken language
- Trouble with saying exactly what you mean
- Trouble with understanding or talking about unfamiliar or abstract subjects
- Trouble with telling an event or story in right sequence

3. Problems in Arithmetic skills – These include :

- Inability to understand the concepts of basic computational skills i.e.addition, subtraction, multiplication and division
- Problems in understanding and applying the concept of place value on worksheets
- Trouble with lining up columns and rows
- Number reversal (for example confusing 6 with 9 or confusing 45 with 54 etc.)
- Problems with understanding the basic signs like +, -, %, >, < etc.
- Problems with concepts of time and direction
- Problems with making change during money transactions
- Problems in balancing accounts
- Problems with keeping scores
- Problems with estimating time, distance, quantity etc.
- Problems with paying attention to problem solving tasks

4. Problems in reading – These include :

- Slow reading speed
- Skipping words or lines while reading

- Reading words or lines out of sequence
- Getting confused in words having same or similar spellings
- Poor vocabulary
- Poor comprehension and recall of information
- Problems in concentrating while reading
- Problem in summarizing what is being read
- Problem in identifying themes or key points in any given article
- Problems in answering open ended questions from any given article
- Problems with organizing and completing written projects/tests

5. Problems in organization – This affects every area of everyday life of the person. Some of the common problems arising out of the lack of organization include :

- Problems with organizing time and following time-table
- Problems with keeping things in order (tend to lose papers, books, keys etc. very often)
- Problem in remembering information including school/office work etc.
- Inability to complete tasks/test papers within the given time frame
- Delay in getting started/procrastination
- Problem in following rules especially during games and sports activities
- Inability to plan things/events/activities

6. Deficit in fine motor skills – Most of the children who have LD also exhibit problems in motor coordination and their fine motor skills are usually

compromised. Commonly found motor problems include :

- Lack of balance
- Problems in writing and drawing including poor handwriting
- Problems in dressing up and grooming
- Problem in playing sports, especially the ones that require aiming and timing

7. Emotional and social problems – These problems are often a result of the other problems but their presence adds up to the problems faced by the sufferer. Few examples include :

- Difficulty in initiating and sustaining conversations
- Inability to make friends and/or sustain friendships
- Problems with social instincts
- Inability to understand body language
- Inability to comprehend social situations and intentions of others
- Inability to belong to any group
- Inappropriate emotional behavior in various social situations
- Inability to cover up ones flaws in public
- Inability to protect themselves from abuse

8. Miscellaneous problems – These include variety of problems which arise out of poor understanding such as :

- Inability to follow and remember directions
- Problems with understanding maps, charts, graphs etc.

- May focus on details and fail to see the bigger picture or may fail to focus on details
- Inability to foresee the consequences of any act

CHAPTER 4

Types of Learning Disabilities

As discussed in the definition of Learning Disabilities in the previous chapter, LD is not a single entity. It includes a wide variety of symptoms in different intensities and combinations in each affected child so that no two children have exactly same problem. However, there is predominance of certain symptoms in a particular child and based on the type of the predominant symptom / difficulty, the scientists have described following types of Learning Disabilities–

1. Dyslexia
2. Dysgraphia
3. Dyscalculia
4. Auditory processing disorder
5. Language processing disorder
6. Non-verbal learning disabilities
7. Visual perceptual deficit

The above classification of Learning Disabilities is as per the description of Learning Disabilities Association of America. This is not absolute or standard. Many other organizations describe fewer types of LDs which is also correct as the problems in each type of LD overlap and co-exist in variable intensities in each person.

4.1 Dyslexia

Dyslexia is a specific learning disability that affects reading and related language-based processing skills. The severity can differ in each individual but it affects reading fluency, decoding, reading comprehension, recall, writing, spelling and sometimes speech. This often exists along with other related disorders. It is a condition where a child is unable to read inspite of having normal intelligence and a will to read. A child suffering from dyslexia commonly shows following signs and symptoms –

- Reads slowly and painfully
- Experiences decoding errors, especially with the order of letters
- Shows wide disparity between listening comprehension and reading comprehension of some text
- Has trouble with spelling
- May have difficulty with handwriting
- Exhibits difficulty recalling known words
- Has difficulty with written language
- May experience difficulty with math computations
- Decoding real words is better than nonsense words
- Substitutes one small sight word for another: a, I, he, the, there, was

Following are few typical pieces of written work by dyslexic children –

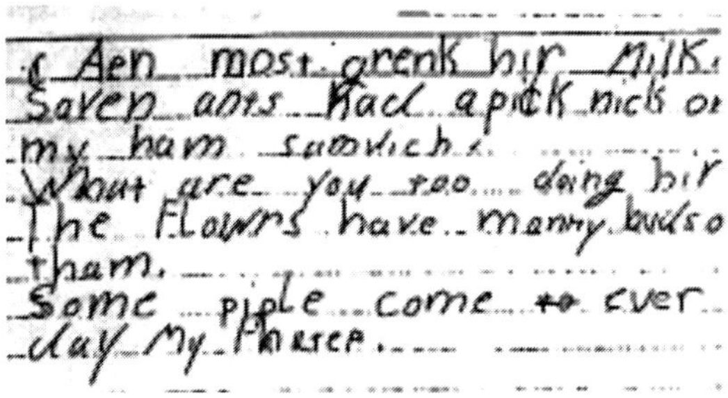

Image1

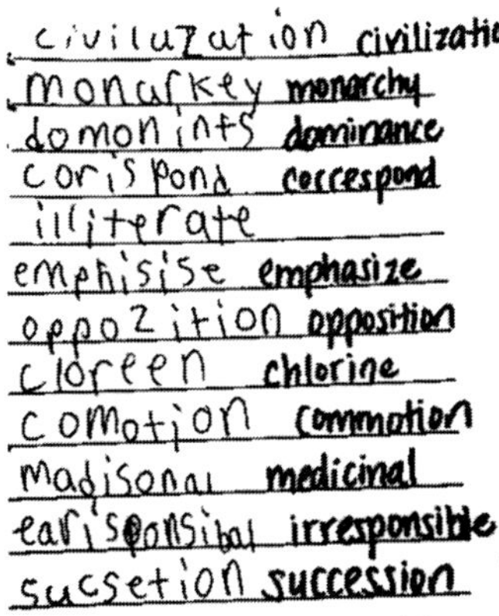

Image 2

4.2 Dysgraphia

This specific learning disability affects a person's handwriting ability and fine motor skills. Problems may include illegible handwriting, inconsistent spacing, poor spatial planning on paper, poor spelling, and difficulty composing writing as well as thinking and writing at the same time. A child with dysgraphia –

- May have illegible printing and cursive writing (despite appropriate time and attention given to the task)
- Shows inconsistencies: mixtures of print and cursive, upper and lower case, or irregular sizes, shapes or slant of letters

- Has unfinished words or letters, omitted words
- Inconsistent spacing between words and letters
- Exhibits strange wrist, body or paper position
- Has difficulty pre-visualizing letter formation
- Copying or writing is slow or labored
- Shows poor spatial planning on paper
- Has cramped or unusual grip/may complain of sore hand
- Has great difficulty thinking and writing at the same time (taking notes, creative writing.)

A piece of writing by a child with dysgraphia may look like following –

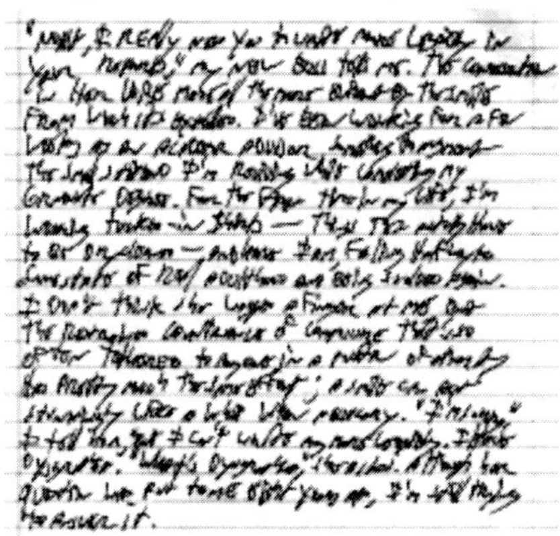

Image 3

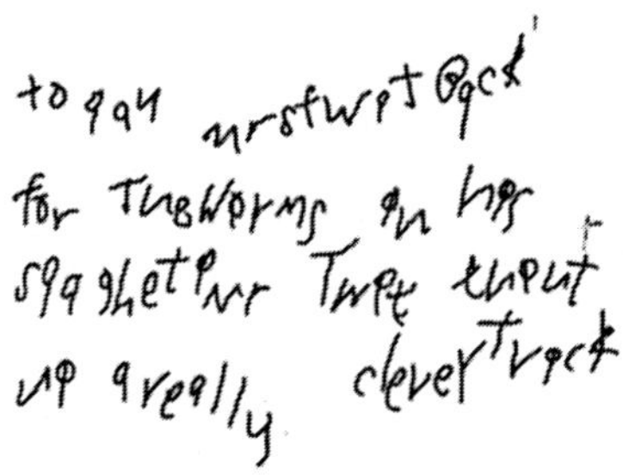

Image 4

4.3 Dyscalculia

Dyscalculia affects a person's ability to do math. A child's ability to do math is dependent on many other abilities and disabilities such as language learning disability, visual disorder or a difficulty with sequencing, memory or organization can lead to poor performance in math. However, dyscalculia refers to the specific problem with memorization and organization of numbers, operation signs and other basic concepts such as fractions, number lines, and positive and negative numbers. This leads to problems in a variety of activities such as –

- Learning to count and recognize numbers.
- Solving basic math problems or memorizing things like multiplication tables.
- Learn basic math, like addition, subtraction, and multiplication
- Organizing problems on the page, keeping numbers lined up, following through on long division problems
- Estimate things, like how long something takes or the ceiling height
- Understand math word problems
- Link a number (1) to its corresponding word (one)
- Understand fractions
- Understand graphs and charts (visual-spatial concepts)
- Count money or make change
- Remember phone numbers or ZIP codes
- Tell time or read clocks
- Understanding concepts related to time such as days, weeks, months, seasons, quarters, etc.

Following diagram depicts the deficit areas and the resultant disabilities seen in persons suffering from dyscalculia –

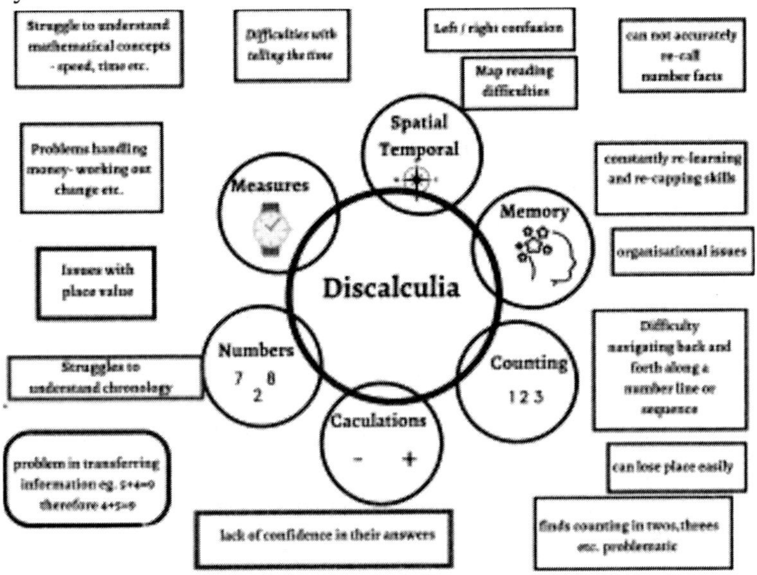

Image 5

4.4 Auditory processing disorder

When the "auditory processing skills" or the "receptive language" or the interpretation of sounds that we hear by the brain is defective, the resultant disorder is called Auditory Processing Disorder or Central Auditory Processing Disorder. CAPD causes inability or decreased ability to recognize subtle differences between sounds in words, even when the sounds are loud and clear enough to be heard. The affected person may also find it difficult to tell where sounds are coming from, to make sense of the order of sounds, or to block out competing background noises. This inability to distinguish subtle differences in sound, or hearing sounds at the wrong speed makes it difficult to sound out words and understand the basic concepts of reading, writing and spelling. It appears as if the person is unable to hear but the hearing tests are normal.

The predominant symptoms arising due to CAPD are –

- Difficulty in processing and remembering language-related tasks but may have no trouble interpreting or recalling non-verbal environmental sounds, music etc.
- Slow processing of thoughts and ideas and difficulty in explaining them
- Problem in spellings and pronouncing similar-sounding words or omitting syllables
- Confusion in similar-sounding words like celery/salary, belt/built, three/free, jab/job, bash/batch etc.
- Poor ability to understand and use figurative language such as using metaphors and similes or inability to understand puns and jokes. The person tends to interpret words too literally
- Too much distraction by background sounds/ noises
- Difficulty in staying focused on or remembering a verbal presentation or lecture or oral directions or directions in a series
- Difficulty in comprehending complex sentences or rapid speech
- Using "What?" too often, even when has heard much of what was said

4.5 Language processing disorder

Language and communication learning disabilities involve the ability to understand or produce spoken language. This is different from an Auditory Processing Disorder because APD affects the interpretation of all sounds coming into the brain (e.g., processing sound in noisy backgrounds or the sequence of sounds or where they come from) while a Language Processing Disorder relates only to the processing of language. LPD can affect expressive language (what you say) and/or receptive language (how you understand what others say). The specific symptoms of LPD are –

- Difficulty in making out meaning from spoken language
- Poor oral and written expression
- Poor reading comprehension
- Difficulty in labeling objects or recognizing labels
- High frustration level because the person has a lot to say and no way to say it
- A feeling that words are "right on the tip of tongue"
- Can describe an object and draw it, but can't think of the word for it
- Difficulty in understanding jokes and other forms of figurative speech
- Inability to retell a story or narrate an event

4.6 Non-verbal learning disabilities

In this type of LD, the affected person has trouble interpreting nonverbal cues like facial expressions or body language and may have poor coordination. The specific characteristic of NVLD is a significant discrepancy between verbal skills and motor, visual-spatial and social skills. The symptoms include –

- Trouble in recognizing nonverbal cues such as facial expression or body language
- Poor psycho-motor coordination, clumsiness, constantly bumping into people and objects
- Compromised fine motor skills leading to problems in tying shoes, writing, using scissors etc.
- Lost appearance and delayed responses (the person usually needs to verbally label everything that happens to comprehend circumstances, spatial orientation, directional concepts etc.)
- Difficulty in coping with changes and transitions
- Difficulty in generalizing previously learned information
- Difficulty in following multi-step instructions
- Making very literal interpretations and translations
- Asking too many questions which may be repetitive and inappropriately timed
- Verbal skills are often strong, imparting an illusion of competence

4.7 Visual perceptual deficit

This is a disorder that affects the understanding or reproducing any information that a person sees. This is characteristically seen coexisting with other types of LDs like dyslexia, dysgraphia or NVLD and it can result in missing subtle differences in shapes or printed letters, poor eye/hand coordination, poor aiming or precision etc. Some of the symptoms observed due to VPD include–

- Frequent letter reversals (e.g. b for d, p for q) or inversions (eg. u for n, w for m)
- Difficulty in negotiating routes and directions
- Frequent discomfort and itching in eyes. The person tends to rub eyes often and complains that the print blurs while reading
- Holding paper at odd angles or keeping head at odd positions while reading
- Inability to copy accurately
- Appears lost frequently
- Inability to recognize an object/word if only part of it is shown
- Holding pencil too tightly and breaking pencil point/crayons too often
- Struggles with cutting and pasting or other craft activities
- The written work may be messy and the letters may appear colliding, spacing may be irregular and the letters may not be on line.

CHAPTER 5

Assessment and Diagnosis

Typically, when a child has problems in reading, writing, mathematics, comprehension or expression, so much so that his overall academic progress is affected, a learning disability is suspected. Sometimes, the only complain is development of behavioural problems in the child. However, once a learning disability is suspected, the first thing is to have an assessment done for the child.

An assessment or evaluation for LD is not a single test. It is a process that involves multiple steps and its ultimate goal is to get a better understanding of the child as a whole. The assessment process aims at gathering all the relevant information about the individual's areas of weaknesses to determine whether or not he or she may have a learning disability. The areas of strength should also be noted down. The components of the assessment process may vary depending on which individual, clinic or agency is conducting the assessment, but most assessments include the following–

- An informal interview or a brief test and review of developmental, medical and school histories.
- Formal testing for achievement, intelligence and information processing.

- Arriving at a diagnosis and documentation of the results of the assessment.
- Recommendations for work, school and/or daily living.

A comprehensive assessment is necessary for children suspected of having a learning disability because it provides detailed information about the child's suspected disability. The data thus obtained is useful in preparing individualized therapy plans for the child and also for monitoring the progress of the child over a period.

5.1 The Assessment Process

An ideal assessment for LD is a long process requiring several sessions with a qualified educational psychologist. Apart from administering a battery of tests, the psychologist also gathers relevant information about the child from the teachers and school records. The assessment procedure for LD involves the following steps –

Step I – Parental Consent and Parental Interview

Parents' consent must be obtained before evaluating the child. The family, academic, developmental and medical history along with details about the linguistic usage and communications patterns of the child must be obtained from the parents. The parent must be involved in the planning of the intervention program.

Step II – Gathering Information from the Teachers/ School

The psychologist must also observe the child in his/ her school setting to know about the child's performance and behavior in the class and gain insights from the teacher. Review of previous grades will show the pattern of academic progress. These may throw light into the problem areas of the child.

Step III – Looking at Student's Workbooks

This may provide valuable information however, in the present educational setup, very often the notebooks don't reflect the learning difficulties faced by the child due to rote learning. The examination papers may give a clearer picture of the specific nature of difficulty. A careful review of the student's school records or work samples help the assessment team identify patterns or areas of specific concern which may be focused on at the time of interview.

Step IV – Interview with the Child

An Interview should be a conversation with a purpose, with questions designed to collect information that relates to the observed or suspected disability of the child.

Step V – Testing

Though increasingly controversial, most assessments for LD include standardized tests. These tests can be of two types –

a) the Criterion referenced tests which are scored according to a standard or a criterion decided by the teacher, the school or the test publisher
b) the Norm referenced tests where the scores are interpreted according to how the student's performance compares with that of his peers.

Essentially, the tests for LD have two major components. One is testing for the discrepancy between potential and performance. This includes testing for intellectual functioning as well as academic achievement of the child. The second component is tests for processing abilities of the child.

Step VI - Evaluation of self-esteem and emotional status of the child

Many students with learning disabilities develop significant problems with self - esteem and show emotional reactions to prolonged frustration. These, in turn, seriously compromise the individual's ability to learn in an effective fashion. Therefore, when such emotional interferences are present, whether as a primary problem or as a secondary reaction to the learning disability, it is imperative that we recognize these as problems and intervene suitably.

5.2 Assessment tools

The purpose of a LD assessment is to accurately identify a student's patterns of strengths and needs. Assessment is critical for making an accurate diagnosis of students with learning disabilities. Procedures that are not comprehensive can result in false positive as well as false negative results. Various LD assessments are guided by following principles -

1. No single data source is sufficient for identifying students with learning disabilities. Data from multiple sources is necessary.
2. A multidisciplinary team of professionals with expertise in learning disabilities, along with the family and may be the student, are necessary to conduct a comprehensive assessment for students suspected of having learning disabilities.
3. Learning disabilities must be differentiated from under-achievement and other types of learning and behavior problems. Under-achievement is common among students with learning

disabilities, but it is not synonymous with learning disabilities.

For a comprehensive assessment and evaluation –

1. A valid and latest version of any standardized assessment test should be used.

2. Multiple measures should be used, including both standardized and non-standardized tests and other data sources such as

- case history and interviews
- evaluations and information provided by parents
- direct observations or data-based information
- standardized age appropriate tests
- curriculum-based assessments, task and error pattern analysis, portfolios, diagnostic teaching and other non-standardized approaches

3. All components of the definition of specific learning disabilities must be considered including all the eight areas of specific learning disabilities i.e., oral expression, listening comprehension, written expression, basic reading skill, reading comprehension, reading fluency, mathematics calculation and mathematics problem solving.

4. The test should examine functioning and/or ability levels across domains of motor, sensory, cognitive, communication and behavior, including specific areas of cognitive and integrative difficulties in perception, memory, attention, sequencing, motor planning and coordination and thinking, reasoning and organization.

LIST OF LD ASSESSMENT TOOLS

The list of LD assessment tools is very long and practitioners have their own preferred tests which they find most suitable. Also, the tests are standardized according to the age group of the child who is to be tested. However, the tests are categorized into following groups -

1. Tests for language (oral and written) - Examples include Assessing Linguistic Behaviours Communicative Intentions Scale (ALB), Clinical Evaluation of Language Fundamentals - fifth edition (CELF-5), Comprehensive Assessment of Spoken Language (CASL), Comprehensive Test of Phonological Processing - second edition (CTOPP-2) etc.
2. Tests for reading - Examples include The Diagnostic Assessments of Reading with Trial Teach Strategies (DAR-TTS), Woodcock Reading Mastery Tests - revised (WRMT-R) etc.
3. Tests for achievement - Examples include Kaufman Test of Educational Achievement, second edition of Comprehensive Form (KTEA-II), Wechsler Individual Achievement Test - second edition (WAT-II), Woodcock-Johnson III Tests of Achievement (WJ III ACH) etc.
4. Tests for intelligence - Examples include Kaufmann Assessment Battery for Children - second edition (KABC-II), Stanford-Binet Intelligence Scales for Early Childhood - fifth edition (Early SB5), Wechsler Preschool and Primary Scale of Intelligence - third edition (WPPSI-III), Woodcock-Johnson III Tests of Cognitive Abilities (WJ III COG) etc.

5. Tests for articulation – Examples include Arizona Articulation Proficiency Scale – third revision (Arizona-3), Goldman-Fristoe Test of Articulation – second edition (GFTA-2), Kaufman Speech Praxis for Children (KSPT), Khan- Lewis Phonological Analysis (KLPA-2), Photo Articulation Test – third edition (PAT-3) etc.
6. Tests for social development – Examples include Ages and Stages Questionnaires : Parent Completed, Child Monitoring System – second edition (ASQ), Vineland Adaptive Behaviour Scales – second edition (Vineland-II) etc.
7. Tests for development of motor skills – Examples include Bayley Scales of Infant and Toddler Development – third edition (Bayley-III), The Beery-Buktenica Developmental Tests of Visual-Motor Integration – fifth edition (Beery VMI), Peabody Developmental Motor Scales – second edition (PDMS-2) etc.

Most of the above tests are standardized according to western population and they are not applicable in Indian scenario. In India, the awareness for learning disability is now increasing and a number of approaches are being used recently for identification and assessment of Learning Disabilities. These include curriculum-based assessment, task analysis, dynamic assessment and assessment of learning style. These approaches yield rich information about students and are especially important when assessing students from culturally or linguistically diverse backgrounds. Following psycho-educational tests are generally used –

1. Intellectual Assessment

2. Achievement or Performance Assessment
3. Assessment of Cognitive Processing Abilities

OTHER ASSESSMENT PROCEDURES

1. Curriculum Based Assessment - Direct assessment of academic skills (Curriculum Based Assessment) is one alternative that has recently gained popularity. Tests of performance in this case come directly from the curriculum. For example, a child may be asked to read from his or her reading book for one minute. Information on the accuracy and the speed of reading can then be compared with other students in the class. CBA is quick and offers specific information about how a student may differ from his peers. Because the assessment is tied to curriculum content, it allows the teacher to match instruction to a student's current abilities and pinpoints areas where curriculum adaptations or modifications are needed. CBA provides information that is immediately relevant to instructional programming.
2. Dynamic Assessment - Dynamic assessment includes a dialogue or interaction between the examiner and the student. This interaction may include modeling the task for the student, giving the student prompts or cues as he/she tries to solve a given problem, asking what a student is thinking while working on the problem and giving praise or encouragement. The interaction allows the examiner to draw conclusions about the student's thinking processes and his/her response to a learning situation.

3. Learning Styles - A learning style assessment attempts to determine the elements that have an impact on a child's learning. Some of the common elements whose assessment may be included here would be the way in which the material is presented in the classroom (i.e. visual, auditory or tactile way), the environmental conditions of the classroom (hot, cold, noisy, light, dark), the child's personality characteristics, the measurements of success that are held by the child and others, the response the child receives (for example, praise or criticism) and the type of thinking the child generally utilizes in solving problems (for example, trial and error, analyzing). Identification of the factors that positively impact the child's learning is very valuable in developing effective intervention strategies.
4. Outcome-based Assessment - Outcome-based assessment involves considering, teaching and evaluating the skills that are important in real-life situations. Assessment, from this point of view, starts by identifying what outcomes are desired for the student. This type of assessment though generally used for the mentally challenged, may also be used for children in the general classroom with severe behavioural difficulties and for the ones who severely lag behind in academics.

So, we can see that the available tools for assessing LD are many but the one common thing is that they all aim at identifying the problem that the child has with the aim of its remediation and that is what is most important.

5.3 Who can assess

Assessment of the learning disabilities usually begins when the parents (or other guardians) or the teachers are worried about the child's learning progress. This is usually followed by the special education teacher's assessment. In cooperation with the class teacher, the special education teacher evaluates whether the child has difficulties in reading, spelling, or mathematics. When the teacher's evaluation seems insufficient and additional help is desired in planning support, the child or adolescent can be referred to the school psychologist, family counselling centre or other suitable agency for further assessment. This further assessment is necessary when

- In spite of diligent work and special education services provided, the child does not learn according to expectations.
- The school's own evaluations and assessments do not seem adequate (for example, there is reason to suspect an extensive problem that the special education teacher's methods failed to assess).
- The school requests assistance in planning appropriate educational support.
- The school requests assistance for smoothing out disagreements between the school and the home.
- Clear regression has occurred in the child's skills.

5.4 Precautions during Testing

While a child is undergoing a comprehensive evaluation, few things must be taken care of such as –

- The tests must be given in the language or form of communication that the child understands best.

- The professional conducting the test must be trained in giving the specific tests and be knowledgeable in the skill area they are testing.
- The evaluation has to gather information about all of the areas of suspected disability.
- The results need to give useful and relevant information that can be used to make decisions about the child's educational needs.
- The conditions must be such which promotes maximum functioning of the child for example there should be no disturbance, child must be adequately rested and physically fit, he should not be rushed etc.

5.5 Using the Test Results for Further Planning

Once the testing is completed, a team of specialists analyses the results and makes suitable recommendations. This includes suggesting minor alterations and adjustments in the child's environment by which the child can learn better. It can also suggest alternative ways of learning such as use of audio-visual aids or it can recommend that the child be given extra time to complete his task. The child may also be allowed use of computer or an assistant during the exams or he may be allowed to take up certain special subject combinations for the exams.

5.6 Emotional Response to Testing

While the assessment process is for the benefit of the child, the child may at times react negatively to the process and develop certain negative emotional reactions such as –

- Confusion – The child may get confused with interviews and so many questions. He may be having questions in his mind about what all this means and what would be the future implications of these tests.

- Anger or frustration – The child may feel like a victim and may think it is unfair to have this or he may get apprehensive that he may not be as successful as his other friends will be. This may bring about anger and frustration in the child and he may behave abnormally.
- Depression or apathy – Despite all the assurances, if the self-esteem of the child is poor, he or she may anyway conclude that he is not good enough or smart enough and this may precipitate depression in the child.
- Denial – Children always want to be like their peers and so, they may not accept the test results. They may not cooperate with the process or the remedial measures if they are in denial of their disability.
- Guilt – Many times, children may feel bad about the added efforts that their parents have to make for their well-being and they may feel that they are a burden on parents and the family. In such cases, the child may have immense guilt over his disability.
- Relief – Many times, the child may feel relief over the diagnosis of disability because of the previous struggles that the child was going through. In such cases, the child may suddenly stop all the efforts towards his studies.

Whatever may be the emotional reaction, it is important for the parents to understand the psyche of the child and take out time to answer all the questions that the child may have and put his mind to rest.

What is most important for the psychologist is to be able to use the available information gathered from the history, clinical interviews, behavioural observations and objective test data to achieve an integrated or holistic picture of the individual and the specific needs for each case. Only with such a well detailed picture of the person as an individual can we begin to specifically identify what type of educational program, supplementary assistance and educational modifications are appropriate for the specific situation. This depicts the importance of the psychological assessment findings. Through such a comprehensive evaluation process, the individual's strengths and talents are also highlighted and brought into focus as a basis for preserving and enhancing self - esteem and personal development.

CHAPTER 6
Theories of Learning Disabilities

6.1 What is learning?

We use the term 'learning' all the time in everyday life. Almost every action we take is the result of learning that happened in the past. As babies, we learn to eat, to gain attention, to crawl, to walk, etc. and as we grow up and our bodies become more functional, we learn a wide range of more complex skills.

Generally speaking, when we use the word "learning", we are talking about a step-by-step process in which an individual experiences permanent, lasting changes in knowledge, behaviors or ways of looking at the world. It is a continuous process that commences at birth and continues until death. The purpose of learning is growth and it is this growth that helps us in dealing with new life situations, developing relationships and leading a happy and useful life.

6.2 How do we learn?

The ability to learn is possessed by humans, animals, plants and some machines. In most of the animal species, learning occurs as a result of classical conditioning, while in other relatively intelligent species, it is a result of more complex activities such as play. Learning may occur consciously or without conscious awareness and it does not happen all at once, but builds upon the previous knowledge.

On a superficial level, learning appears to be a simple task and involves the process of moving information from a textbook, a report or an audio/video to the inside of our heads and making that knowledge our own. But the fact is that learning is not so simple. Most of us must have experienced that there are times when we read, we memorize and we practice and still the information doesn't stay inside our heads. On the other hands, there are times when we are exposed to a fleeting piece of information and it stays with us forever.

6.3 Various theories of learning

It has been found that cognitive, emotional and environmental influences, as well as prior experience, all play a part in how understanding or a world view is acquired or changed and knowledge and skills retained. A number of elaborate theories have been put forward by psychologists over the ages that try to explain the process by which these external influences get incorporated within our neurological system thereby causing the 'learning'. These 'learning theories' are conceptual frameworks describing how information is absorbed, processed and retained during learning. Some of the main theories of learning are –

1. **Classical Conditioning Theory** – This theory was majorly the result of the work of Russian physiologist Ivan Pavlov. Classical conditioning theory involves learning a new behavior via the process of association. In simple terms two stimuli are linked together to produce a new learned response in a person or animal. Classical conditioning occurs when a conditioned stimulus is paired with an unconditioned stimulus. After pairing is repeated, the organism exhibits a conditioned response to the conditioned

stimulus when the conditioned stimulus is presented alone.

2. Operant Conditioning Theory - Operant conditioning was first described by the behavioral psychologist B.F. Skinner. It is also called as Instrumental conditioning. Like classical conditioning, operant conditioning also relies on forming associations. In operant conditioning, however, the associations are made between a behavior and the consequences of that behavior. When a behavior leads to a desirable consequence, it becomes more likely that the behavior will be repeated again in the future. If the actions lead to a negative outcome, however, the behavior then becomes less likely to occur.

3. Cognitive Theory of Learning – This theory was put forward by Jean Piaget, a Clinical Psychologist from France. According to Piaget, children are born with a very basic genetically inherited mental structure on which, all subsequent learning and knowledge is based. Cognitive development occurs by a progressive reorganization of mental processes as a result of biological maturation and environmental experience. Children construct an understanding of the world around them. They then experience discrepancies between what they already know and what they discover in their environment and this leads to further learning.

4. Social Learning Theory – This theory was put forward by Albert Bandura and it is in accordance to the experiential learning as described in classical conditioning and operant conditioning model of learning. However, it says that learning does not always happen by experiencing. Many times, we observe what is going on around us within our social set-up and learn things through these observations. Bandura believes that humans are active information processors and analyze the relationship between their behavior and its consequences. Therefore, individuals do not automatically observe the behaviour of a model and imitate it. There is some thought prior to imitation and this consideration is called mediational processes. This occurs between observing the behaviour (stimulus) and imitating it or not (response).

6.4 Factors affecting learning

As is evident from above, there have been continuous attempts to understand the learning process with an obvious aim to improve it, thereby improving the functional capacity of any human being. It is during these studies that psychologists have also come across a variety of factors that affect learning. Some of these factors are –

1. **Intellectual Factors –** This refers to the individual's innate mental capability with which he or she is born with. It is predominantly genetically determined.

2. **Motivation –** Studies say that communicating information is necessary but not the only condition for a workable knowledge to be created. The success of the learning process ultimately depends on the how well the learner imbibes an information and this inclination to imbibe and absorb any information is automatically created within the person by the expected benefit that he or she is expecting from learning a particular information or skill. Intrinsic motivation has a more powerful and long lasting effect on learning than extrinsic motivation.

3. Physical and Mental Maturity - Physical and mental maturity makes the learning speedy. A structurally and functionally mature system can process information in much better way as compared to an immature mind and body system.

4. Home Conditions and School Environment - When students' basic psychological needs of safety, belonging, autonomy and competence are satisfied at home as well as at school, they are more likely to perform better and contribute to the community in positive ways. Along with the psycho-emotional factors, the physical environment of the home and school also affect learning to a huge extent. Lighting, ventilation, acoustics of the rooms and building design classifications such as flexible classroom arrangements, clearly defined pathways, positive outdoor spaces etc. also affect the learning of the students.

5. Teacher's personality - The way a teacher's personality interacts with the personalities of the students determines the kind of behavior which emerges from the learning situation. Effective teaching results from the teacher's love for the students, sympathy for their interests, tolerance and a definite capacity for understanding. The supreme value of a teacher lies in his power to lead and to inspire his pupils through the influence of his moral personality and example.

6. Teaching Methods- - Effective teaching strategies help to activate students' curiosity about a class topic, engage students in learning and develop critical thinking skills. They keep students on task and encourage sustained and useful classroom interaction and in general, enable and enhance the maximum learning of course content.

6.5 Theories of Dyslexia

The primary symptoms of dyslexia were first identified by Oswald Berkhan in 1881 and the term 'dyslexia' was coined in 1887. Since then, researchers have been investigating what exactly dyslexia is and trying to identify its biological causes. Many theories have been put forward to explain the occurrence of the condition and to make one understand the variety of symptoms found in the condition.

It must be kept in mind that various theories are an attempt to complete the jigsaw puzzle of the complex problem of dyslexia. No theory is complete in itself but if seen together in synergy, they offer a satisfactory explanation for the array of symptoms of dyslexia.

The various theories describe dyslexia at three levels–

1. **Behavioural theory** - These describe dyslexia at the level of changes observed in the behavior of the person affected. The theory considers reading, writing, rhyming skills etc. as individual acquired behaviours that are learnt by people with age and exposure. And it says that the learning disability arises due to a failure to acquire these behaviours.

2. **Cognitive theories** - These describe dyslexia in terms of deficit in processes involved in cognition. These predominantly include -

   a) Phonological deficit theory

   b) Visual deficit theory

   c) Automaticity deficit theory

3. **Biological theories** - These describe the dyslexia in terms of changes occurring in the structure and function of brain. A number of biological theories have

been put forward on basis of observations in various groups of children and adults affected by dyslexia. These mainly include –

a) Cerebellar deficit theory

b) Magnocellular deficit theory

Behavioural Theory

This describes dyslexia as a disorder in which a child shows certain specific behavioural abnormalities such as –

1. Problem in reading and writing
2. Problems with number skills
3. Speech and language problems
4. Problems with attention such as ADD, ADHD, high distractibility, problem in switching from one mental activity to the other etc.
5. Problems in motor coordination, fine motor skill development, balance etc.

This is the most primitive theory of dyslexia and holds no significance anymore.

Phonological Deficit Theory

The phonological module of dyslexia argues that dyslexics have impaired reading ability because they have a deficit in phonological processing. According to this model, dyslexic people experience difficulties in reading and understanding written language because they have an impaired ability to deconstruct written words into phonemes, thus preventing word identification. This low level of phonological awareness prevents words from reaching high levels of linguistic processing, which would allow the reader to gain meaning from the text. Thus, dyslexics have intact memory and comprehension language processes that are not activated because they can only be activated after a word has been identified through phonological processing. The phonological model of dyslexia explains why dyslexics have difficulty with reading while remaining intellectually capable of processing very complex thoughts and ideas.

The basic hypothesis is that dyslexia stems from a functional or structural deficit in left hemispheric brain areas associated with processing the sounds of language. In the past two decades, the phonological deficit theory has been the dominant explanation of dyslexia, but it is only one of several competing theories. Critics of the phonological theory point out that it fails to account for symptoms of dyslexia unrelated to phonetic decoding difficulties, such as problems with short-term memory, visual processing issues or difficulties with balance and motor coordination that are common to many dyslexic children and adults. They also argue that much of the evidence for the theory is based on reasoning and that phonological weakness is seen as both a defining symptom of dyslexia and as its underlying cause.

Visual Deficit Theory

The Visual deficit theory considers dyslexia as a visual impairment giving rise to difficulties with the processing of letters and words on a page of text. This may take the form of unstable binocular fixations, poor convergence or increased visual crowding. The visual theory does not exclude a phonological deficit, but emphasizes a visual contribution to reading problems, at least in some dyslexic individuals. At the biological level, the visual system is divided into two distinct pathways that have different roles and properties: the magnocellular and parvocellular pathways. This theory states that the magnocellular pathway is selectively disrupted in certain dyslexic individuals leading to deficiencies in visual processing, and, via the posterior parietal cortex, to abnormal binocular control and visuo-spatial attention. Evidence for magnocellular dysfunction comes from anatomical studies showing abnormalities of the magnocellular layers of the lateral geniculate nucleus, psychophysical studies showing decreased sensitivity in the magnocellular range, and brain imaging studies.

Automaticity Deficit Theory

This theory states that dyslexic children have problems in fluency for any skill that should become automatic with extensive practice.

A group of researchers found that dyslexic children had severe problems with a wide range of skills, including balance, motor skills, phonological skills and rapid processing. Many of these skills were not language based, suggesting that the phonological deficit could not explain all the problems in dyslexia. Looking at all the data together, they inferred that most of the children showed problems in multiple functional areas rather than with different specific skills such as audiological or visual processing. They found out that the dyslexic children had problems in ability to switch attention and had difficulty in orienting attention. This, in turn, was found to be a result of having problems in the automaticity of shape recognition and spatial working memory, especially when the processing demands were high. This theory is supported by the fact that the dyslexic children show an improvement in their performance when they are trained for attention orienting.

Cerebellar Deficit Theory

Cerebellum is an area at the base of the brain which is known to be associated with motor skill development, especially the balance and coordination. This has evolved enormously so that it is not only linked with the motor areas at the front of the brain, but is also linked with some areas further forward in the frontal cortex, including Broca's language area. The cerebellar theory of dyslexia asserts that a mildly dysfunctional cerebellum can cause dyslexia. This theory was initially proposed by Harold Levinson and Jan Frank in 1973.

The cerebellar theory is based largely on the association of dyslexia with a lack of balance, coordination and time estimation as well as the cerebellum's suggested role in modulating memory, concentration, communication and emotional skills and sensory integration. Additional research has shown that those with dyslexia show impairments in both the right and left sides of their cerebellum, including a lower than normal blood-flow to these regions while performing tasks the cerebellum is responsible for. Those with dyslexia can also exhibit earlier delays in motor milestones associated with the cerebellum, such as crawling, walking, talking, and coordination. Direct evidence of cerebellar deficit in dyslexia came from a PET scan study which revealed that dyslexic adults did not show the normal pattern of activation when performing a motor sequence learning task.

Magnocellular Deficit Theory

In order to read, it is important to be able to sequence letters in the right order. Correct letter sequencing depends on a group of neurons called the magnocellular (M) system. These M neurons form 10% of the ganglion cells in the retina and they are specialized for timing visual events by sensing movement rather than form or color. M cells also project via the magnocellular layers of the lateral geniculate nucleus (LGN) in the thalamus to the primary visual cortex in the back of the occipital lobe and also to the superior colliculus to control eye movements. The axons of M cells are heavily myelinated so that the signals they project to the visual cortex arrive there approximately 10 ms before the slower ones provided by other cells. These magnocellular neurons are also present in auditory afferent pathways and are responsible for understanding of rapid auditory stimulus.

The magnocellular theory of dyslexia proposes that the people with dyslexia have abnormalities of the magnocellular pathways and hence, they are unable to process fast incoming sensory information adequately in any of the three domains i.e phonological, visual and motor domains.And this leads to emergence of various symptoms of dyslexia. This hypothesis is supported by various anatomical, electrophysiological, psychophysical and brain-imaging studies in different groups of people by different researchers.

In summary, all the theories account for at least some of the symptoms of dyslexia, but none of the theories completely explain the array of symptoms Found in the children with dyslexia. The deficits they predict have been found in varying percentages of dyslexic children and these deficits are observable in brain scans.

The need to have clarity about the origin of dyslexia

is that the intervention techniques can be planned accordingly. If we go by the cerebellar deficit theory, we must include the balance training and fine muscular coordination training in the remedial plans. If we go by the phonological deficit theory, the training will mainly be for aural comprehension skills. However, since we do not have any clear cut information about the causation of dyslexia, the remedial programs generally include training for all the probable areas where deficit can occur.

CHAPTER 7

Management of Learning Disabilities

Learning disabilities are treated educationally, preferably with early intervention. The best way to understand and treat learning disabilities is head on, with targeted screenings and assessments, and focused intensive and explicit instructions. There are many different treatments that are being advertised as "effective," and it is best to consider them carefully before investing time and money on them. In case the child has an superadded attention disorder, medication can be helpful. ADD and ADHD cannot be cured but can be controlled with medication and even more effectively with a combination of medicine, behavioral therapy and educational support.

The three step process of managing LDs include –

- The first step is "demystification" which involves counseling the child and family so that they are able to understand the nature of the learning difficulty and the steps needed to make progress. Demystification relieves shame and promotes self-esteem and positive coping strategies.
- The second step is direct remediation of LD which typically requires intensive 1-on-1 instruction with a special education teacher, and a lot of encouragement from parents and teachers. Progress needs to be monitored

carefully to better understand what works best for each child.

- The third step is developing bypass strategies so that the child can progress with the curriculum despite his/her challenges. For example, a child with dyslexia may benefit from extensive use of video and other media for learning, one with dysgraphia may need a scribe or voice recognition software for some written assignments and one with dyscalculia may need to use a calculator extensively.

7.1 Few specific strategies for handling different types of LDs

- For dyslexia –
  - Provide a quiet area for activities like reading and answering comprehension questions
  - Use books on tape
  - Use books with large print and big spaces between lines
  - Provide a copy of lecture notes
  - Don't count spelling on history, science or other similar tests
  - Allow alternative forms for book reports
  - Allow the use of a laptop or other computer for in-class essays
  - Use multi-sensory teaching methods
  - Teach students to use logic rather than rote memory
  - Present material in small units
- For dysgraphia –
  - Suggest use of word processor

- Avoid chastising student for sloppy, careless work
- Use oral exams
- Allow use of tape recorder for lectures
- Allow the use of a note taker
- Provide notes or outlines to reduce the amount of writing required
- Reduce copying aspects of work (pre-printed math problems)
- Allow use of wide rule paper and graph paper
- Suggest use of pencil grips and / or specially designed writing aids
- Provide alternatives to written assignments (video-taped reports, audio-taped reports)

- For dyscalculia –
  - Allow use of fingers and scratch paper
  - Use diagram and drawings for math concepts
  - Provide peer assistance
  - Suggest use of graph paper
  - Suggest use of colored pencils to differentiate problems
  - Work with manipulatives
  - Draw pictures of word problems
  - Use mnemonic devices to learn steps of a math concept
  - Use rhythm and music to teach math facts and to set steps to a beat
  - Schedule computer time for the student for drill and practice

- For auditory processing disorder –
    - Show rather than explain
    - Supplement with more intact senses (use visual cues, signals, handouts, manipulatives)
    - Reduce or space directions, give cues such as "ready?"
    - Reword or help decipher confusing oral and/or written directions
    - Teach abstract vocabulary, word roots, synonyms/antonyms
    - Vary pitch and tone of voice, alter pace, stress key words
    - Ask specific questions as you teach to find out if they do understand
    - Allow them 5-6 seconds to respond ("think time")
    - Have the student constantly verbalize concepts, vocabulary words, rules, etc.
- For language processing disorder –
    - Speak slowly and clearly and use simple sentences to convey information
    - Refer to a speech pathologist
    - Allow tape recorder for note taking
    - Write main concepts on board
    - Provide support person or peer tutor
    - Use visualization techniques to enhance listening and comprehension
    - Use of graphic organizers for note taking from lectures or books

    - Use story starters for creative writing assignments
    - Practice story mapping
    - Draw out details with questions and visualization strategies
- For non-verbal learning disabilities –
    - Rehearse getting from place to place
    - Minimize transitions and give several verbal cues before transition
    - Avoid assuming the student will automatically generalize instructions or concepts
    - Verbally point out similarities, differences and connections; number and present instructions in sequence; simplify and break down abstract concepts, explain metaphors, nuances and multiple meanings in reading material
    - Answer the student's questions when possible, but let them know a specific number (three vs. a few) and that you can answer three more at recess, or after school
    - Allow the child to abstain from participating in activities at signs of overload
    - Thoroughly prepare the child in advance for field trips, or other changes, regardless of how minimal
    - Implement a modified schedule or creative programming
    - Never assume that the child understands something because he or she can "parrot back" what you've just said

    - Offer added verbal explanations when the child seems lost or registers confusion
- For visual perceptual deficit -
    - Avoid grading handwriting
    - Allow students to dictate creative stories
    - Provide alternative for written assignments
    - Suggest use of pencil grips and specially designed pencils and pens
    - Allow use of computer or word processor
    - Restrict copying tasks
    - Provide tracking tools: ruler, text windows
    - Use large print books
    - Plan to order or check out books on tape
    - Experiment with different paper types: pastels, graph, embossed raised line paper

An educational specialist can teach effective learning strategies to help a child overcome his or her learning problems. It is also essential to provide opportunities for success in areas where the child may shine. Interventions vary depending on the nature and extent of the disability. Getting help earlier increases the likelihood for success in school and later in life. If learning disabilities remain untreated, a child may begin to feel frustrated with schoolwork, which can lead to low self-esteem, depression and other problems.

7.2 Treatment of associated conditions

Apart from educational difficulties, children with learning disabilities have one or more associated problems such as ADD, ADHD, motor dyspraxia, speech difficulties and emotional and social problems etc. Suitable treatment for these conditions is needed to ensure overall well-being and progress of the child. Speech therapy, physiotherapy, occupational therapy, counseling and behavior modification regimes are helpful in overcoming the above mentioned problems. Medical treatments are available for ADD and ADHD but they too work best in conjunction with supportive therapies.

7.3 What experts say

Candace Cortiella, a parent and professional working with disabilities in Washington D.C. says that parents should be cautious about treatments that are promoted as a cure for learning disabilities. While some medical interventions (such as medication if a child has also been properly diagnosed with a coexisting disorder such as ADHD) can be most helpful, many treatments are unproven and ineffective. Many of the treatments that we see being promoted through advertising are extremely costly and have no independent research showing that they are effective and that the effects are sustained over time. Should parents find a treatment that looks promising, a substantial amount of homework should be done before proceeding for it. Parents can be quick to act on a promising treatment, wanting to help their child if at all possible. Keeping in mind that a learning disability is a life-long condition that can't be "cured" will help parents make wise decisions.

Dr. Gail Grodzinsky, a professional psychologist and counselor working with children having learning disabilities in California says that any well-researched treatment recommended by a trained and qualified professional is likely to have some merit. There is rarely just "one" intervention that will have an impact on a child with a learning disability. Often, a multidimensional treatment plan works best. For example, while a reading-disabled child will clearly benefit from explicit instruction in word decoding, comprehension skills and exposure to literature should also be considered. "Cure" therapies, including computer software, one-size-fits-all reading programs, restricted diets, special glasses, etc. must be viewed with extraordinary caution and cynicism. The "whole" child must be considered in any treatment plan. Sometimes, it is necessary to prioritize treatment components. For example, structuring the classroom environment before a medical approach is used can be helpful in some cases.

Dr. Cheryl Weinstein, a clinical neuropsychologist working in Massachusetts, says that multiple interventions that look after the biological, psychological and social factors of the disease are essential and comprise a general principle of treatment. We all want that magic bullet to take care of learning problems. Unfortunately, the belief that medication alone will work is too readily embraced. Likewise, the belief that behavioral strategies alone are enough contains both risks and benefits. When family members say "Oh... no meds... no meds," I might say, "If your child had diabetes, you would run for insulin treatments" or "If your child had heart disease, you would be at hospital immediately to get medications." When parents agree with my statements, I then ask, "Can you explain why the pancreas and the heart require medication and the brain does not?" This is a crucial issue because there is an unfortunate assumption that brain-based functions are controlled by "will and motivation" rather that brain structure, brain interactions, and neurotransmitters, etc.

The most important treatment, however, may simply be someone helping the child/adolescent/young adult accept who they are and determine the best ways to move on. A young man who was evaluated for LD recalled that his teacher had told him that his "brain didn't work quite right with all of his internal supports, but, when he used external supports, he moved at a high level and all his great ideas came together." He spent the rest of his education developing those external supports, and what he has achieved is admirable. He held on to the thoughts expressed by his teacher because she believed in him and gave him hope for the future.

CHAPTER 8
Supporting Children with Dyslexia in Indian Context

Research indicates that perhaps 10 to 15% of children may suffer from some type of Dyslexia. In our country, this figure may be even larger since multilingualism can also impact on the difficulties that a child faces in learning spoken and written language. Since these children with special needs are also a part of our society, it is our duty to give them the necessary support wherever needed and include them within our system. Without this support, they will not be able to sustain themselves in the existent system. Also, since their intelligence level is normal to high and many of them have exceptional talents, if we leave them without support, they will get marginalized and we will lose manpower resource.

Broadly speaking, the support that these children require must be at three levels–

1. Family support – The prime responsibility of the family in case of dyslexic children is to make sure that their emotional status remains high. Family must also act as an advocate for the child and ensure that the child gets all which is rightfully his, atleast until the child learns to take up his responsibility and be his own advocate.

2. Institutional support - The school, colleges and the institutions offering employment to these candidates must first understand the specific needs of the person and then cooperate with the person as far as possible.
3. Support at the organizational level - The policy-makers should provide the necessary clauses so that inclusion in the mainstream is assured for the children with dyslexia.

8.1 Family Support

The first institution of a child where he learns is his home. A child passes most of his time with his parents and learns from his parents and the environment provided to him by his parents at home. Parents play a vital role in the education of their child, whatever child's age is. If parents pay adequate attention to their children, the children learn and grow up well. This responsibility becomes even greater if the child has special educational needs.

The first step in the education of a special needs child is to become aware that he has a special need. Some children are identified very early in their lives as having life-long special needs while some children start school and it then becomes apparent that they are having difficulty in learning.

Ideally, the first step to take as a parent is to talk to the teacher and decide together what needs to be changed in order to improve the child's learning. If minor classroom changes are not able to bring the desired changes, it is necessary to have a more in-depth assessment of the child to identify his special learning needs by a psychologist. Whatever may be the opinion of the psychologist, one important thing that every parent must remember is that if they don't accept the diagnosis and hide the facts from the teachers, all they will do is lose the valuable time that can otherwise be utilized for betterment of the child. Ofcourse, they may seek second or third opinion regarding the diagnosis if in doubt or they may take help of a counselor in order to manage their emotions, but acceptance of the situation realistically is important and the sooner it is accepted, the better is the outcome for the child.

However, dyslexia is a new entity for our society in general. Very few people, including those involved with academics, are aware of the term dyslexia. And many of those who have heard of the term dyslexia are unaware of the exact nature of the condition. Under such conditions, we can't expect that a child with dyslexia can get support from even his family and friends. The parents and the child keep struggling with their difficulties and this struggle is at multiple levels such as –

- The parents usually don't have a clue as to why their child is poor in studies when he/she can perform well in all other areas. They generally end up punishing the child rather than supporting him.
- Even if the parents know that their child has dyslexia, they are not aware of what exactly is meant by this term and what the needs of this child are.
- The right kind of support and therapies are scarce except in metro cities and so, the frustration level in the parents of special children becomes very high so much so that they get disheartened and

then can't support the child inspite of having the intention.

- The parents who are well aware and laborious also get disheartened during the course because although the government has made the rules, our beaurocratic system is such that it is a huge struggle to claim the facilities that are promised by the government to a dyslexic child.

Not just this, parents of special needs children in India undergo a constant mental churning. At every step, they have to choose between with what is ideal, how much they can handle or afford in terms of money and time and what they desire. These decisions are very tough in our existing social system where every person is fighting a battle for existence and survival at his or her own level. As a result, they tend to continuously reanalyze their decisions again and again. And in this process, a lot of time is lost which could otherwise have been used for the child's development. So, it is important that the parents stick to what they have decided and wait for a reasonable time before revising their decisions. Also, there is social stigma associated with disabilities and so, the parents have to struggle to keep their and the child's morale high in spite of the social compromises they have to make.

Once the course of action has been decided, the training of the child starts as per the chosen plan. The training may take place in regular schools or in special schools by a regular or a special education teacher. But in each case, parent has to be the anchor for the child's education. Unless the parent is involved, no teacher or educator can educate a child with special needs, the level of involvement that a parent can have may vary as per the parent's capabilities, availability of time and his willingness. He may choose to just be informed about what is being done with the child. Or he may take active interest in all the activities going on with the child in the school and help in preparing the child for various activities. Or parents may exchange their views with the school management, participate in dialogue and insist upon getting various facilities for their child at school. Parents may also get involved in IEP formation for their child if they are aware enough of the process. Or they may come forward and take-up the responsibility to teach various skills to their child in order to facilitate the development.

Inspite of all the shortcomings of our existing system, conscious involvement of parents in a special child's education is best for the child because of the following reasons –

1. Parents know their children best. They know their likes and dislikes, their strengths and needs, their abilities and challenges.
2. No one can match the sincerety level that a parent has for the welfare of his child.
3. If parents function in coordination with the teachers, the rate of development can be hastened.
4. A child can stay with a teacher for few hours only hours. Rest of his time is spent at home, with parents. So it is obvious that parents can teach the child much more than any teacher can do.
5. Even if the parents don't actually teach skills, if they are conscious enough to provide a nurturing environment to the child, the job of the teacher becomes much easier.

6. Parents are the ones who can build a good self-image in the child.
7. Since the children with special needs generally have a coexisting communication difficulties, parents can also act as their social advocates and help people listen to the child's voice.

Parenting a special needs child is a tiresome and ongoing task and there are certain things that parent of a special needs child has to do so that he can fulfill his responsibilities. These-

1. Keeping oneself physically and mentally fit
2. Gathering knowledge about the child's disorder and what needs to be done for it
3. Updating the knowledge
4. Be in constant communication with the school and the teachers and therapists of the child.
5. Keep a realistic view about life as a whole
6. Be connected to other parents and seek support when needed and give support when others need.
7. Be aware about the rights of the child
8. Be an advocate of the child and help him get what he rightfully deserves
9. Get the specialized help for the child whenever advised or when the need is felt

Thus, we can say that in our Indian context, whatever the special needs child learns mostly depends on the efforts taken by the parents and their determination and perseverance towards the betterment of their child.

8.2 Institutional Support

Inspite of their differences, all children are equal and hence deserve equal opportunities and equal exposure.

With this in mind, the schools and educational institutions must provide a classroom where the normal children and special needs children sit and study together. Such a system is called inclusive education system.

Studies have shown that when a child with special educational needs attends classes along with other children, the results are good. But it is also true that simply making the two types of children sit together cannot produce positive outcome. An ongoing effort has to be put in to make this setup a success. Continuous advocacy, planning, support and commitment are needed for making an inclusive education setup successful.

There are three basic principles on which inclusive education is based. These are –

1. All children are equal - Inclusive education is based on the simple fact that all children are "children" first and "children with disability" later. And hence, they all deserve same opportunities and experiences.
2. All children learn in different ways – Inclusive education is based on the fact that every child, whether normal or whether a child with a disability, is unique and has a unique style of learning. Inclusion is about building friendships and developing partnerships so that the children help each other learn. The role of a teacher is to provide help when and where needed, and that too, only as much as needed.
3. It is every child's right to be included – For a long time, children with special educational needs were either neglected or educated in

separate classes or separate schools. But, inclusive education is every child's right, not a privilege as per the laws.

The key benefits of inclusive education are –

- All parents want their children to be accepted by their peers, interact with them and lead a normal life and this dream can come true only within inclusive education setups.
- Mutual respect and understanding grows when children with different abilities and cultures play and learn together.
- Children learn to appreciate diversity and develop a broader view about the world when they see their classes which reflect the similarities as well as the differences of people.
- In an inclusive education setup, children with disabilities get to interact with their normal peers and thus develop social skills that benefit them throughout their lives.
- Inclusive setup is beneficial for self-esteem of both the normal and the special needs child. Special needs child feels good about himself because he is being accepted by everyone whereas normal children feel good about themselves as they feel they have done good work by helping their friend with a lesser ability.
- Inclusive setup is good for academic learning too. The normal children learn better while helping their lower ability friend learn things whereas the lower ability children learn better because they can relate better to their peers rather than to their teachers.

- Since children learn best by imitating, special needs children learn other skills better too in inclusive setup because they have their normal peers as role models.

However, present education system in India focuses more on scores rather than knowledge. Schools put kids under a lot of pressure to perform well in exams rather than focusing on acquiring knowledge and their overall development as a human being. The educational institutions have a huge competition among themselves and each institution wants to prove that it is the best by giving best results and in this process, they put the children under immense performance pressure. Under these conditions, we can hardly expect these institutions to act on humanitarian grounds and direct their resources towards providing the necessary support to the children with special needs.

8.3 Support at the organizational level

The Indian government has been very considerate towards the needs of the children with disabilities, including those with dyslexia. Some of the major policies include –

1. The Right to Free and Compulsory Education Act [2010] – This act states that right to education is a fundamental right of all and Indian Government will ensure free and compulsory education to all children aged 6-14. The clause no. 4 and 9(g) of this act makes it obligatory on local government to provide education to children which includes the children with disabilities.

The flaw in this act was that its beneficiaries technically include the children with disabilities who fall in any one of the 7 categories of disabled people defined in the Person With Disability Act (PWD) of

1995. But this act mentions only seven disabilities and "specific learning disabilities" is not one of them. As a result, SPLD children fall into the "general" category and are not given the facilities required for their education.

2. The Rights of Persons with Disabilities Bill [2012] – The PWD Act of 1995 has been revised by the ministry of social welfare. The new bill has included SPLD / Learning disability in its list of the types of disabilities. This is the first time that SPLD has found place in national draft policy.

3. A Comprehensive Plan of Action for Children and Youth with Disabilities was presented by the Human Resource Development Ministry in March 2005 which advocates inclusive education, and envisages making all schools "disabled-friendly".

Legislation in favour of inclusion has also been supported by circulars issued by various state and central boards of education, such as the CBSE (Central Board of Secondary Education) and the ICSE. These circulars list various concessions that children with disabilities can avail of. In a circular issued in May 2005, the CBSE states that children with disabilities should have "barrier-free access to all educational facilities", and that dyslexic students can study one language instead of two and any four of the subjects such as mathematics, science, social science, music and painting, among others. The ICSE provides extra time to students with disabilities to complete exams, as well as writers, if required. The children can also choose from a number of subjects such as yoga and physical training.

Several state governments have similar policies for

their boards. The Maharashtra board, for instance, gives students with disabilities extra time during tests, concessions while learning mathematics and the option of studying one language less than what is otherwise mandatory.

8.4 CBSE Guidelines for the Children having Dyslexia

As per the Central Board of Secondary Education, all children with disabilities are allowed compensatory time as follows –

- For paper of 3 hours, extra duration is 60 minutes.
- For paper of 2 hours 30 minutes, extra duration is 50 minutes.
- For paper of 2 hours, extra duration is 40 minutes.
- For paper of 1 hours 30 minutes, extra duration is 30 minutes.

In addition, these children can get a scribe appointed for them by the Board.

The children are also exempted from studying the third language from class VI to VIII. In class IX-X, they have the option of studying one language instead of two. For other four subjects, they have a wider choice and they can opt for more practical subjects like music, painting, home-science etc. Also, if the child is undergoing physiotherapy exercises, it is considered to be equivalent to the Physical and Health Education course of the board.

In addition, Board provides separate question papers in enlarged prints in the subjects of Mathematics and Science if requested.

For the dyslexic students of class XI-XII too, there is

an option of taking music, painting and home-science as subjects of study.

Board has also given following guidelines regarding the special needs children to all the schools which are registered with the board –

1. Ensure that no child with special needs is denied admission in mainstream schools.
2. Provide support to the special needs children through assistive devices and the availability of trained teachers.
3. Modify the existing infrastructure to meet the needs of all children with special needs.
4. Ensure regular in-service training of the teachers in inclusive education at the elementary and secondary level.
5. Revise classroom organization to suit the needs of the children of special needs.

Board has 10 regional offices which ensure that these guidelines are followed by the schools in their respective regions. Board also has a special helpline service which is functional on all working days from 9 AM to 7 PM.

Similar provisions are provided by few other state boards such as Maharashtra Board.

8.5 Actual Scenario

Following facts portray the actual scenario for the children with special educational needs in India –

- At present, in India, the concept of Dyslexia is limited to few big cities only.
- Even Directors of State Education are known to express doubts at the existence of any such disability.

- The teachers are not trained to identify developmental/learning disabilities.
- There is a scarcity of professionals trained to diagnose dyslexia and provide proper interventions.
- Most of the (research and intervention) work in the area of LD is being done by private organizations and the NGOs and there is little communication between these organizations and the state educational authorities.
- The multilingual social context and early age of formal schooling makes the early diagnosis even more difficult.
- While majority of people in our country are still struggling to fulfill their basic needs, it is impossible for them to afford the expenses of remedial therapies
- Our educational system, with its overwhelming emphasis on knowing rather than learning, theory rather than application, is ill-suited for the child with LD.

The most significant evidence of the neglected state of the services provided for the children with dyslexia is that we don't even have a data that can show their status!

CHAPTER 9

Prognosis of Learning Disability

It is very natural that after a child is diagnosed with learning disability, the parents are anxious to know the long term implications of the diagnosis. They are concerned about the future of their child but unfortunately, longitudinal studies of the outcome in adulthood of childhood learning disability are lacking. Also, expecting or concluding a particular outcome from the available evidence is unreliable.

However, there have been some outcome studies in learning disability. Early studies focused mainly on morbidity and mortality (e.g. Decker and colleagues, Richards and Sylvester), while more recently the emphasis has shifted towards systematic consideration of quality of life.

Studies of the outcome of childhood learning disability have adopted a variety of strategies. Various outcome measures have been used such as -

(1) General health
(2) Adaptive functioning
(3) Psychopathology
(4) Life expectancy
(5) Financial independence
(6) Integration into adult life.

9.1 General health

It is very difficult to collect data related to health of the children with learning disabilities due to multiple factors. For long, learning disabilities were either undiagnosed or were grouped along with various other types of mental disabilities so whatever data is available is nonspecific. Also, since these disabilities occur and present themselves as a spectrum of problems, it is not possible, and not justified also, to attribute any particular health issue to presence of learning disability.

Research suggests that there are a number of health conditions that people with a learning disability are more likely to experience, including:

1. Being underweight or overweight – Bhaumik et al. (2008) estimated that men with a learning disability are 8 times more likely to be underweight than those in the general population, and women with a learning disability are 2 times as likely. Two other large-scale studies estimate that the proportion of adults with a learning disability who are underweight is between 14 and 18.6% (Emerson 2005; Gazizova et al. 2012). Being underweight was found to be associated with -

- relatively profound learning disabilities
- younger age at the time of diagnosis
- not taking medication for mental health, behavioural or sleep problems (Bhaumik et al. 2008; Emerson 2005).

Rates of obesity of between 21 and 27% have been found in adults with a learning disability in the UK, which is similar to the rate of obesity in the general population (Bhaumik et al. 2008; Emerson 2005; Gazizova et al. 2012). However, research shows that certain factors are associated with higher levels of obesity amongst people with a learning disability, including:

- being female
- having a milder learning disability
- having co-existing Down's syndrome or Prada-Willi syndrome
- having a co-existing mental health problem (Emerson 2005; Goldstone et al. 2001).

2. Dementia - The rate of dementia is high in all people with a learning disability, but it is particularly high in people with co-existing Down's syndrome. It is documented that the rate of dementia in adults with a learning disability aged 65 and over, not including people with Down's syndrome, is nearly 5 times the rate of the general population (Strydom et al. 2013). People with Down's syndrome have an even greater chance of developing dementia, and at an earlier age. An Irish study found that 15.8% of over 40s with Down's syndrome had dementia or some other serious memory impairment (McCarron et al. 2011). This compares to 6% of over 60s in the general population of Ireland (Pierce et al. 2014). Research also suggests that increased prevalence of dementia amongst people with a learning disability may be due to environmental effects. It has been found that engaging in cognitively stimulating activities at a later age can help stop dementia from developing. As people with a learning disability are less likely to be engaged such activities than the general population, it is possible that this has a negative impact on their cognitive functioning (Strydom et al. 2013).

3. Epilepsy - Research indicates that epilepsy is more prevalent in adults with a learning disability than those without a learning disability; and is more common amongst men and those with a higher level of impairment (Joint Epilepsy Council of the UK and Ireland 2011; McGrother et al. 2006). Research also suggests that people with a learning disability who have epilepsy are significantly more likely to exhibit behaviour problems than those without epilepsy (McGrother et al. 2006).

4. Respiratory disease - People with a learning disability have higher rates of respiratory disease (19.8%) than the general population (15.5%), with respiratory disease causing 50% of deaths of people with a learning disability. This is a particular risk for people with severe learning disabilities who are immobile or underweight.

5. A report says that people with learning disabilities have proportionally higher rates of gastrointestinal cancer than the general population. It accounts for 48% of cancer related deaths as compared to 25% of cancer related deaths in the general population.

6. People with a learning disability have higher rates of gum disease, calculus and caries than the general population

7. Cardio Vascular Heart (Disease) is associated with obesity and with some syndromes

8. There is an increased risk of thyroid disorders in people with Downs Syndrome and some association with anti-epileptic mediation and genetic syndromes.

9. Less than 10% of adults with a learning disability

eat a balanced diet with sufficient intake of fruits and vegetables.

10. About 30% of people with learning disabilities have a significant sight problem

11. 40% of people with learning disabilities have significant hearing problems.

9.2 Adaptive functioning

Adaptive functioning is one of the major concerns of the parents of children with learning disability. In other words, they are concerned whether the child will acquire necessary skills and be able to function normally.

There are many factors that powerfully influence acquisition of adaptive functioning in children with learning disability. These include –

1. There is good evidence that the severity of learning disability in childhood is predictive of subsequent poor social adaptive functioning. Clarke and Clarke, in their study, concluded that early severe learning disability very powerfully predicts long-term dependency and disability.

2. Presence of conduct disorder during early years is also an important adverse factor that predicts poor outcomes in terms of adaptive functioning.

3. Presence of concomitant health issues such as epilepsy, malnutrition etc. also indicates a poor prognosis.

4. More recent reviews emphasized that a host of environmental variables are also crucially important. These include poor parenting, non-supportive environment etc.

It has been found that children with learning

disability attain maximal social adaptive functional outcome through carefully programmed intervention. Hatton and colleagues demonstrated that specialized community-based care models do seem to generate optimal global outcome. However, it has to be kept in mind that learning disability is a condition that cannot be cured. The child has to live with it throughout his or her life. He or she may be specially trained to acquire various skills and lead a productive life.

9.3 Psychopathology

About 30% of learning disabled children exhibit behavioral and emotional problems, which range from attention deficit hyperactivity disorder (most common) to oppositional defiant disorder, conduct disorder, depression, anxiety, suicide etc., to substance abuse (least common).It has also been found that psychopathology worsens with age in children with nonverbal learning disabilities.

Some of the observations on basis of various studies include –

- Learning disability and autism are synergistic and their co-existence exacerbates the symptoms of each other.
- If the symptoms of learning disability are observable at an early age (in 0- to 3-year-old children), the chances of developing behavioural problems in later life are very high.
- Male children having learning disability are more prone to develop psychological and behavioural problems. They are also more prone to indulge in antisocial and criminal acts.
- Few non-child factors such as family criminality, poverty and adverse parenting also predict a

poor outcome in terms of developing subsequent psychopathology.

9.4 Life expectancy

In a major review, Harris and Baraclough found that learning disability was associated with a death risk 2.8 times higher than expected, and the mortality risk from unnatural causes was 3.1 times higher. Seventy-eight percent of deaths among the people with learning disability were from unnatural causes, while only 22% were from natural causes. In general, children with learning disability have a shorter life expectancy than other children. There are studies that have clarified that mortality increases with increasing severity of learning disability. Other high risk factors which predict or are associated with earlier death in people with learning disability include any additional physical disability or medical problem, notably cerebral palsy and poorly controlled epilepsy. Non-mobile children and those incapable of self-feeding are especially at risk of short life expectancy. Causes of death among people with learning disability include respiratory infections, arterial disease, status epilepticus, cancer and accidents.

9.5 Financial independence

Our current social scenario is highly competitive and it is quite obvious that the people whose performances are compromised in one or the other way are sure to suffer. It must always be kept in mind that the nature and severity of learning disability will exert a substantial influence on the person's working and financial independence. It is difficult for them to find good jobs since their academic records and qualifications are usually not very good. Even if they find a suitable job, it is difficult for them to sustain those jobs because of compromised social skills, planning skills, coping and problem solving skills etc.

Studies have found a direct correlation between the degree of motivation and participation by the families and sustaining the employment in people with various types and degrees of learning disabilities. Nature of the work assigned and the work place environment also influence the outcomes. If the jobs are chosen in accordance with the skills and interests of the individual and the environment is supportive, the chances of positive outcome become much higher.

9.6 Adjustment to adult life

For the parents of children with learning disability, the most passionately held hope is that the child will enjoy a satisfying, fulfilling and successful adult life.

The available follow-up studies indicate that while many individuals do enjoy a so-called successful and fulfilling life, we still do not have a very optimistic data when it comes to studies related to key indicators of adult such as employment, relationships, criminality and adult mental health. However, the data show that in respect of most outcome indices of general integration into adult life, the child with more severe disabilities is at greater risk. The studies have also found out that the outcomes for children with mild learning disability have improved in more recent years. Encouraged by such observations, Tizard perceived that the outcome and situation of people with mild learning disability have improved so much and it must only be a matter of time before the same improvements would apply to the situation of children with more severe learning disability.

In summary, it is not entirely possible to predict definitive adult outcomes for an individual child with learning disability. There are certain key issues that influence the outcome such as -

- The severity of childhood learning disability in terms of IQ exerts a major influence on subsequent development and adjustment.
- The presence of any major physical disability has a substantial bearing on outcome.
- Self-perception, parental and family factors and wider societal influences are important mediators of the key biological variables.

Practically, therefore, the task is to identify opportunities for intervention in these various domains in order to promote maximal outcomes for children with learning disability.

CHAPTER 10
Parenting a Child with Learning Disability

From the moment parents become aware of their child's learning disability, another dimension is added to the family system. While the child's problems are often most apparent at school, they do have a reflection at home and quickly become a family problem in every sense. A variety of emotional and practical issues arise and they need proper handling. There are additional responsibilities for parents such as medical and educational decisions, financial pressures and time constraints. The typical emotional response to the child's problem such as inherent concern, disappointment, anger, shame and blame also contribute to the pressures and are frequently disruptive to the family equilibrium.

10.1 The grief cycle

Whenever a person confronts a really bad news or faces a severe loss, he or she undergoes a series of negative emotions. It was found that there is largely a pattern in the series of emotions and this series is called grief cycle. The stages in the grief cycle are -

- Shock stage - This is the initial short period when the person goes numb after hearing the news.
- Denial stage - In this stage, individuals believe

the diagnosis is somehow mistaken, and they tend to cling to a false, preferable reality. This phase may extend for years in few cases when the parents either keep ignoring the problems or they run from one specialist to another in a hope of getting a favourable diagnosis.

- Anger stage - This is the stage of frustrated outpouring of bottled-up emotions, especially at proximate individuals. Certain psychological responses of a person undergoing this phase would be "Why me?", It's not fair!", "How can this happen to me?", "Who is to blame?", "Why would this happen?" etc.
- Bargaining stage - This is the stage when the sufferer realizes the truth but seeks for a way out in unrealistic ways. For instance, the person might think "I'd give anything to make the child alright." Or "If only my child becomes alright, I'd promise to be a better person!" Or "I'll never scold the child again, God please make him normal again!"
- Depression stage - This is the stage when the person finally realizes the true magnitude of the problem and it depresses him or her. He may isolate himself from others and reflect upon the past to find a reason for what is happening. Or, there may be a sense of emptiness, despair and hopelessness. He may feel incapable and powerless due to a total loss of control over the situations.
- Acceptance stage - This is the stage when the person finally comes to the terms with the situation. It does not mean that he is happy in

the situation or that he does not want the situation to change. It merely means that the person finally accepts the reality and starts thinking about the ways to handle it and starts planning the life accordingly.

- Testing stage - This is the stage when the person starts overcoming the negativity and begins to explore for practical ways to handle the situation. He starts developing new perspectives about life and finds newer strengths and new goals.

It is not necessary that every person goes through these phases in the same order. The emotions keep fluctuating and many times, especially when there is inadequate support and inappropriate guidance, parents are not able come out of this emotional cycle and lead a unfulfilling life themselves. This situation is worsened by the fact that frequently the mother and father may be involved in different and conflicting stages at the same time (e.g., blame vs. denial; anger vs. guilt). This can make communication very difficult. In extreme cases, this might act as a catalyst to dissolution of the marriage.

10.2 Implications on the family

Having a child with disability in the family has profound effects on the entire family. On the positive side, it can broaden horizons, increase family members' awareness of their inner strength, enhance family bonding and encourage connections to religious groups and promote spiritual growth of each member of the family. But on the negative side, the time and financial costs, physical and emotional demands and managing all the household affairs in accordance with the additional demands associated with raising a disabled child can have multifold effects. These effects depend on the type and severity of the condition as well as on the overall resources of the family.

Some of the effects on the parents include –

- They usually suffer from mental and physical stress
- There is difficulty in finding appropriate and affordable child care
- Either or both the parents have to make compromises in their career
- Parents' social life may suffer
- Parents may have to compromise in their self-care due to financial limitations
- All the decisions about the future are affected such as planning for better job or another child or a new home etc.

- Relationship between the two parents and that with the extended family might also become strained.

Although very little is specifically known about how the siblings are affected by presence of the disabled child, some effects that have been observed include –

- Behavioural aberrations and poor social adjustment in younger siblings due to negative role model exhibited by the disabled child.
- Aberrations in the personality of the sibling because he/she has to make compromises throughout
- Poor long term mental health outcomes due to relative neglect from the parents who are busy with the disabled child

Another potentially important but under-explored area is how child's disability affects the well-being of grandparents and other extended family members and how the responses of those individuals to having a disabled child in the family affect the child's parents. Overall, much more needs to be learned about how children's health affects their parents, siblings, grandparents, and extended family members.

10.3 Parenting tips

Few people realize how difficult it is to be a parent until they become a parent themselves. Parents are totally responsible for the safety, welfare and education of a tiny infant who quickly becomes a growing, ever-changing and maturing child. Parents have to set their own rules, develop their own routines and form their own expectations. And if it is difficult to be a parent, it is even more difficult to be a parent of a child with special needs. Broadly speaking, following are some of the additional tasks that a parent of a special needs child must do –

- Managing their own emotions – It is said that the earlier we start the intervention, the better is the development of the child. So, the parents can't and shouldn't waste much time in struggling with their own emotions. It is important that they find a suitable outlet for venting out and managing their emotions.
- Gathering knowledge – It is a must for the parents to read and talk about the problem with right people in order to find out more about the nature of the problem and the best possible resources available for the remediation.
- Understanding behaviours – Since the children with learning disability often exhibit a variety of emotional and behavioural problems, it is important that the parents try to understand why the child is doing whatever he is doing. Unless they do this, they will either over-react or under-react to the odd behaviours. Also, if the behavior correction strategies are planned without understanding the basic reason behind the behavior, desired results will not be achieved.
- Acting as an advocate for the child – Special needs children have to face hurdles at every step, especially in developing countries like India. So, it is the responsibility of the parents (and of siblings later on!) to stand up for the rights of the child at each step. This is even more

important if the child has a limitation in self-expression.

- Addressing the difficulties with time and space – Since the children with learning disabilities usually have difficulties in organizing and planning, the parents have to constantly support them in managing their belongings and their time.
- Addressing relationship difficulties – These children also lack social skills very often and hence have a problem in initiating and maintaining relationships. So, the parents have to assist them at each step in maintaining friendships.
- Promoting self-esteem – The children usually know, either objectively or instinctively, that they lag behind their peers in one or more skills and this leads to a poor self-esteem. As is usual, they don't realize that the deficiency is in some particular area of development. They generalize it and the usual thoughts are of being "incapable", "inadequate", "not good enough", "undesirable" etc. and with a poor self-esteem, their performances will further decrease. So, it is the responsibility of the parents to make them realize their strengths as well as in a realistic way and restore their self-esteem.
- Empowerment – These children usually lack coping and problem solving skills. This, along with a poor sense of spatial organization, makes the child feel powerless. And this feeling makes the child dull and laid-back which again has a

negative effect on the child's learning. The parents need to support them and teach them the basic life skills so that they regain their power and zeal.

Some specific tips for the parents include –

- Take the time to listen to your children as much as you can (really try to get their "message").
- Love them by touching them, hugging them, tickling them, wrestling with them (they need lots of physical contact).
- Look for and encourage their strengths, interests, and abilities. Help them to use these as compensations for any limitations or disabilities.
- Reward them with praise, good words, smiles, and pat on the back as often as you can.
- Accept them for what they are and for their human potential for growth and development. Be realistic in your expectations and demands.
- Encourage healthy lifestyle habits.
- Encourage independence.
- Involve them in establishing rules and regulations, schedules, and family activities.
- Tell them when they misbehave and explain how you feel about their behavior; then have them propose other more acceptable ways of behaving.
- Help them to correct their errors and mistakes by showing or demonstrating what they should do.
- Don't nag!
- Give them reasonable chores and a regular family work responsibility whenever possible.

- Give them an allowance as early as possible and then help them plan to spend within it.
- Provide toys, games, motor activities and opportunities that will stimulate them in their development.
- Read enjoyable stories to them and with them. Encourage them to ask questions, discuss stories, tell the story, and to reread stories.
- Enhance their ability to concentrate by reducing distracting aspects of their environment as much as possible (provide them with a place to work, study and play).
- Don't get hung up on traditional school grades! It is important that they progress at their own rates and be rewarded for doing so.
- Take them to libraries and encourage them to select and check out books of interest.
- Have them share their books with you.
- Provide stimulating books and reading material around the house.
- Help them to develop self-esteem and to compete with self rather than with others.
- Insist that they cooperate socially by playing, helping, and serving others in the family and the community.
- Serve as a model to them by reading and discussing material of personal interest. Share with them some of the things you are reading and doing.
- Don't hesitate to consult with teachers or other specialists whenever you feel it to be necessary in order to better understand what might be done to help your child learn.

10.4 Aim for life success rather than school success

In general, for most of the people, a successful life means having satisfying relationships and a fulfilling job that earns good money. Success is also a relative term and one is considered to be successful if he or she is better, or projects to be better than the most of the other people around him or her. In case of children, the school grades, as compared to other children, are the marker of being successful. However, with a learning disabled child, the family has to change its perspective and the meaning of "success". Few newer ways of thinking can be –

- Instead of focusing on comparison with others, the focus should be on constant self-improvement.
- Instead of focusing on grades, the focus should be on attaining knowledge and practical skills.
- Instead of focusing on academic skills, focus on teaching practical life skills, such as problem solving, willingness to ask for and accept help, determination to keep trying despite repeated failures, ability to form relationships etc., to the child.
- While choosing careers, instead of choosing socially acceptable careers, one should go for the careers which suit the skills and interests of the child.
- Instead of focusing on the salary, the focus should be on job satisfaction.

A 20-year study that followed children with learning disabilities into adulthood identified six attributes that possibly determine success in life. If the parents focus on these broad skills, the likelihood of having a successful life is increased many times. These include–

1. Self-awareness and self-confidence –For children with learning disabilities, self-awareness (knowledge about strengths, weaknesses, and special talents) and self-confidence are very important. Struggles in the classroom can cause children to doubt their abilities and question their strengths. Few tips for promoting self-awareness and confidence include -

- Ask your child to list his or her strengths and weaknesses and talk about your own strengths and weaknesses with your child.
- Encourage your child to talk to adults with learning disabilities and to ask about their challenges, as well as their strengths.
- Work with your child on activities that are within his or her capabilities. This will help build feelings of success and competency.
- Help your child develop his or her strengths and passions. Feeling passionate and skilled in one area may inspire hard work in other areas too.

2. Being proactive - A proactive person is able to make decisions and take actions to resolve problems or achieve goals. For people with learning disabilities, being proactive also involves self-advocacy (for example asking for a seat at the front of the classroom) and the willingness to take responsibility for choices. Few tips for encouraging the child to be proactive include –

- Talk with your learning disabled child about problem solving and share how you approach problems in your life.

- Ask your child how he or she approaches problems. How do problems make him or her feel? How does he or she decide what action to take?
- If your child is hesitant to make choices and take action, try to provide some "safe" situations to test the water, like choosing what to make for dinner or thinking of a solution for a scheduling conflict.
- Discuss different problems, possible decisions, and outcomes with your child. Have your child pretend to be part of the situation and make his or her own decisions.

3. Perseverance - Perseverance is the drive to keep going despite challenges and failures, and the flexibility to change plans if things aren't working. Children (or adults) with learning disabilities may need to work harder and longer because of their disability. To encourage perseverance -

- Talk with your learning disabled child about times when he or she persevered—why did he or she keep going? Share stories about when you have faced challenges and not given up.
- Discuss what it means to keep going even when things aren't easy. Talk about the rewards of hard work, as well as the opportunities missed by giving up.
- When your child has worked hard, but failed to achieve his or her goal, discuss different possibilities for moving forward.

4. The ability to set goals - The ability to set realistic and attainable goals is a vital skill for life success. It also involves the flexibility to adapt and adjust goals according to changing circumstances, limitations or challenges. To encourage this –

- Help your child identify a few short- or long-term goals and write down steps and a timeline to achieve the goals. Check in periodically to talk about progress and make adjustments as needed.
- Talk about your own short- and long-term goals with your child, as well as what you do when you encounter obstacles.
- Celebrate with your child when he or she achieves a goal. If certain goals are proving too hard to achieve, talk about why and how plans or goals might be adjusted to make them possible.

5. **Knowing how to ask for help** – Strong support systems are key for people with learning disabilities. Successful people are able to ask for help when they need it and reach out to others for support. For this –

- Help your child nurture and develop good relationships. Model what it means to be a good friend and relative so your child knows what it means to help and support others.
- Demonstrate to your child how to ask for help in family situations.
- Share examples of people needing help, how they got it, and why it was good to ask for help. Present your child with role-play scenarios that might require help.

6. **The ability to handle stress** – If children with learning disabilities learn how to regulate stress and calm themselves, they will be much better equipped to

overcome challenges. In order to teach this –

- Use words to identify feelings and help your child learn to recognize specific feelings.
- Ask your child what words they would use to describe stress. Does your child recognize when he or she is feeling stressed?
- Encourage your child to identify and participate in activities that help reduce stress like sports, games, music, or writing in a journal.
- Ask your child to describe activities and situations that make them feel stressed. Break down the scenarios and talk about how overwhelming feelings of stress and frustration might be avoided.

All this is easier said than done. Most parents use almost every resource they have to help their child flourish but the results are not always as per the expectations. It is all too easy for parents to sense the child's feelings of inadequacy and then feel bad as a parent. But truth is that this is not going to help in any way. However, clear and concise instructions, structuring of the atmosphere without rigidity, nurturing the child's gifts and interests and constant approval of positive behavior does help. It takes time for both children and parents to embrace the concept that being different does not mean being inferior. And last but not the least parents too need to be nurtured and praised to help them nurture and praise their children.

CHAPTER 11
Living with Learning Disability

For the teachers, parents and all other persons concerned with a child having learning disability, the main concern is to provide suitable support to the child so that the normalcy in the life can be restored as far as possible. But for the children suffering with learning disability, this is a condition with which they have to live. They have to face restrains and setbacks at multiple levels every day. And for them, the biggest challenge is to manage the emotional burden that comes with such a situation and still keep trying.

11.1 What the kids with learning disability feel during their childhood

The child is struggling to perform well at more than one front. Like all other children, they have a desire to be appreciated and recognized and there is a natural desire to be the best. But most of the times, even their near and dear ones fail to understand these needs and desires. To add on to this, these children, most of the times, have poor ability to express themselves. The result is a frustrated child and this frustration further deteriorates the performance level. Some of the commonly experienced emotions include –

1. "I wish I was smarter!" – Though most people have a feeling that kids want to play, look good, have a good friend circle, have lots of fun and have nice things

to eat. But the truth is that deep inside, single basic desire of every child is to learn and be very smart. And they need recognition from their parents and teachers that they indeed are smart. So, it's no wonder that when kids don't do well in school, even when given extra help, they feel dumb. They get embarrassed, frustrated, and angry with themselves for not succeeding.

2. "I know my mother is keeping secrets from me and I don't like it when people talk behind my back." - Once a child is identified with a learning disability (LD), the changes that occur at home and school seem endless. It's very clear to kids when they're not told the whole story about their learning struggles. They don't feel included in conversations about their learning difficulties, both at home and school. In a way, they feel like things are being done "to" them and not "with" them. They get pulled out of classes, taken out of familiar schools, and spend extra time on schoolwork instead of participating in fun activities like their siblings and peers.

3. "No one knows what I'm going through."- Kids in general feel alone in their experiences, but kids who are struggling to learn feel even more isolated. They feel like no one understands them. Struggling in school is definitely not a topic they would bring up with other people, especially their friends, for fear of being made fun of them. "It would feel good to talk to my family and friends about my learning because then I wouldn't feel out of place anymore. But I know I can't."

Although there are no set rules to manage these emotions, some useful tips include –

1. Praise, praise, praise - The child needs to be recognized and encouraged for things that he can do

well. If the child has some exceptional talent, encourage and applaud it. If no such talent has been identified, make an effort to give him praise for the little things he does. For example for helping in household chores, for sitting for studies without reminding, for keeping his things neatly etc. When you take notice, you'll see that these opportunities are around every corner.

2. Talk to your child - For parents it's natural to try to protect kids from life's harsh realities. But the truth is that the kids suspect the worst if parents don't talk to them. The more open and honest you are with your child, the more trust he'll have in your relationship. Let him know that you're going to get through this together. Include him in as many family meetings and appointments with professionals as possible. Tell your child what to expect in the meetings and talk about them afterwards to get his opinion on how it went. Simply, speak the unspoken to the child and both the child and the parent will benefit.

3. Encourage your child to talk - Let the child know and believe that you're available to listen to him and promise not to make judgments about what he tells you. Acknowledge his emotions without telling him what to feel and what not to feel. Share your own childhood experiences of the times you might have felt bad or embarrassed about yourself. This lets him know that he's not alone. Your behavior should give him an assurance that you understand what he's going through.

11.2 From childhood to adulthood

The focus during childhood is mainly on improving the child's performance. As the child grows up and becomes an adult, the focus shifts on having practical life skills. An adult is supposed to sustain himself well and live an independent life. For a person with learning disability, this sustenance is not possible without external support. The kind of support they need include –

- *Support at home* – Persons with learning disability might need support in managing their daily needs such as in cooking, managing clothes etc. Apart from this, the biggest support that the family can give is in managing the emotions. The person with learning disability has to face setbacks at every step but the world outside will not care about his emotions. It is at home only where he can take the liberty of expressing himself and release the emotional burden which otherwise suffocates him.
- *Transport* – These persons often have problem with directions and hence might need help with their transportation.
- *Leisure opportunities* – Due to deficient social skills and poor ability of self-direction, these persons might not find suitable opportunities for recreation by themselves and hence need support.
- *Financial support* – If the person is not suitably employed, he will need financial support to manage his expenses.
- *Advocacy* – Persons with learning disability usually need support for self-advocacy to assert their rights and claim what is rightfully theirs.
- *Employment* – Persons with learning disability usually need help in acquiring and sustaining employment due to their deficient or compromised working and behavioural skills.

11.3 Equipment and adaptations

Learning disabilities can't be cured but with the help of specific gadgets and tools, a child with a learning disability can work around his or her difficulties with reading, writing, numbers, spelling, organization or memory. Tools help people of all ages with learning disabilities reach their full potential, giving them greater freedom and independence along the way.

Tools for people with learning disabilities can be simple things such as highlighters, color coding files or drawers, books on tape, tape recorders, calculators or a different paper color or background color on a computer screen. Or, it may be complex highly technical gadgets such as –

- Computers that talk to help people with reading and writing difficulties,
- Speech recognition systems that turn oral language into written text,
- Talking calculators that assist people with math difficulties, and
- Computer software that can predict words for people with spelling difficulties.

CHAPTER 12
Learning Disability in Real Life

12.1 Few case notes

Case 1

A 5 year old boy was brought for evaluation since he was asked to repeat class in school. The teacher's complaints were inability to listen and follow directions, inappropriate social behaviour when playing with other children and handwriting delays. On observation, the child was found to ignore teacher's requests, was unable to stay on task and lashed out at other children when over stimulated. His handwriting showed frequent letter reversals. Although the child did not listen to his teacher, when placed in calm environment, he exhibited a high motivation to perform. On assessment, the child was found to have dyslexia with autistic features. With specific training and behavioural management strategies, the child started showing improvement.

Case 2

A 5 year old boy was brought for consultation because of difficulty in concentrating and very poor pencil holding and writing skills. On taking history, the parents admitted that the child has poor motor functioning at home too and has to be helped with his daily activities like dressing, eating etc. On examination, the child was found to have deficient fine and gross motor skills. The muscle tone was poor, especially in the trunk muscles and the sensory development was not up to the mark. Sense of balance and position were especially deficient. The concentration problem was due to the restlessness arising out of the poor sensory integration. With appropriate physical and sensory integration therapies, along with few modifications in the environment of the child, the problems started regressing.

Case 3

A 7 year old boy is very poor in reading and writing. Parents feel that he is not interested in studies and so, always finds reasons to avoid studying. He is exceptionally active and is virtually always on move. On observation, the child has difficulty in following orders and avoids direct gaze due to very poor confidence level. His writing is slow and labored and there are many letter reversals and many letters are out of sequence. His mathematic skills are also poor and he gets distracted very easily. On examination, the boy has difficulties with body awareness and sound processing. The sense of balance is also impaired. Testing reveals clinically significant difficulties with starting tasks, working memory and planning & organization. The child showed improvement with sensory integration therapy, modified reading strategies and other strategies to enhance word and number identification etc.

Case 4

Parents of a 7 year old girl were regularly getting complains from the child's school that she doesn't complete her classwork, remains lost and also doesn't take interest in games and other co-curricular activities.

Parents also felt that she doesn't follow instructions properly and they assumed that she doesn't pay attention to what is being said to her. They also found her to be very clumsy in her movements and attributed this to her being careless. However, on examination, the girl was found to have difficulties with processing sound. Her body awareness, emotional control and working memory were also not good. With proper therapeutic support, the symptoms resolved to a great extent within a short period and the girl became much more active and confident.

Case 5

Mother of a 10 year old boy brought him for assessment since the child was not able to cope with the increasing academic pressure. His work was often unfinished and the handwriting was so poor that it was often impossible to make out what he has written. On assessment, it was found that the child had poor fine motor skills and poor pencil grip. No other significant problem was found. On taking history, it was found that the child was a little slow since beginning but he could manage his school work. He lost his father about 2 year back. After that, the mother had to take up the family responsibilities so she too could not give quality time to the child. As a result, the child became very irritable. This added upon his basic motor deficiencies and further deteriorated his performance. Due to constant scolding by the teachers, he had developed a negative association with them and this resulted in a severe lack of interest and motivation. With suitable support and appropriate behavior management techniques, the child improved drastically.

Case 6

A 7 years old girl was brought for consultation with a complaint of lack of concentration which was leading to poor academic and behavioural performance at school. On assessment, the child was found to have specific learning disability and this was the reason for poor performance, inability to concentrate and increased irritability. With suitable modifications in teaching strategies and additional support at school as well as home, the child showed improvement. One to one sessions for boosting self-esteem and identifying the specific areas of strength and weaknesses were also conducted and proved very helpful in making the parents and teachers understand the child well.

Case 7

A 7 year old boy was referred for assessment by the school authorities. His writing was totally illegible. When he started writing, one or two lines used to be readable. After that, whatever he wrote, even he could not make out later. It was hard for him to sit in his place during class and in groups, his movements became too much and uncontrollable. He wanted to be included in all activities but when he was asked to perform, he tended to get very anxious and could not do anything. On examination, the child was found to have sensory integration issues, especially of visual and auditory processing and vestibular control which lead to poor bilateral coordination of body movements. The muscle tone was weak, especially in the trunk. This created an inner restlessness which reflected as hyperactive behaviour. He was asked to do specific physical exercises to improve trunk strength and rhythm and timing of muscular movements. Self-regulation awareness training about his "body speed" and breathing and thinking tools to calm him down were also prescribed. Direct handwriting training including self-monitoring to build strength, endurance and legibility were also recommended. All the symptoms significantly regressed within 6 months of starting therapy.

Case 8

A 6 years old boy was brought for assessment because of difficulties in maintaining attention, poor handwriting, poor posture and decreased ability to attend to a given task. On examination, the child was found to have difficulty in co-ordinating the movements of the two sides of his body, poor motor planning for gross and fine motor skills and poor postural tone and control. The child was also over-responsive to movement input. This was linked to poor processing of vestibular and proprioceptive information. Neurodevelopmental treatment and sensory integration techniques were used to address postural issues, bilateral integration, vestibular and proprioception processing issues and his sensitivity to vestibular input. Fine motor concerns were addressed using a variety of craft activities involving deep pressure. The child improved with the therapies but for substantial improvement, long term intervention is needed.

Case 9

A 6 year old boy was brought for consultation because of poor handwriting and poor motor skills. The child was found to have delayed gross motor and fine motor development. With appropriate sensory motor therapy plan, the child improved. His handwriting as well as the writing speed improved and he could complete his class work. His participation in outdoor games also increased and he could relate well with his peers.

Case 10

A consultation was sought for a 5 year old boy who had difficulty in completing school work and could not make friends with other children. He also had frequent emotional outbursts, feeding difficulties and sensory seeking behavior. The examination revealed an auditory processing difficulty, low registration of sensory information, oral sensory difficulties, low muscle tone and immature pencil grip. The parents and teachers were educated regarding the problem and were asked to implement a timetable strictly. Suitable sensory motor intervention was delivered simultaneously. The child showed improvement but sustained improvement requires long term therapy.

Case 11

A 9 year old girl was brought for consultation due to anxiety, depression, poor working memory and attention. She was struggling with her academics and was a year behind her peers at school. She had high activity level and had difficulty in sitting still in class. At home, she needed help for bathing, toileting and using spoon while eating. She had to be accompanied during sleeping. On examination, she was found to have moderate sensory processing difficulties, hypersensitivity to sound, poor body awareness and impaired whole body movement processing. Visual processing skills, attention and working memory were also below average. In academics, she was below grade level for most subjects and specially lagged behind in spelling skills. A variety of therapies were started simultaneously for her improvement. Sensory integration therapies with strategies to retrain her auditory and vestibular processing skills were started. Visual perceptual and motor integration trainings were started. Parents and teachers were educated regarding origin of her behavioural issues so that they can understand what she needs when she is behaving in a particular way. Yoga and breathing exercises were introduced for self-calming and reduction of anxiety. Cognitive exercises for improving comprehension, memory and problem solving were also started. The child took time to show improvement but within a year, her performance at school improved and she was excelling in her preferred sport - gymnastics.

Case 12

A 18 years old boy was brought for consultation due to severe disinterest in studies. He also had a lot of behavioural issues such as frequent lying, stealing money from her mother's purse, not listening to his parents and not fulfilling any responsibility at home. On examination, it was found that the boy had mild dyslexia due to which, he was not able to cope up with his studies. But since his parents were not aware of existence of any such disorder, they kept on thinking that he was being inattentive and irresponsible and so tried to control him by scolding sometimes and giving him undue support at other times which resulted in development of severe defiant behavior. Also, to hide his frustration and failure, he adopted a habit of telling lies and spending money on his peers to gain their acceptance. With proper counseling of the boy and the family, the behavioural problems reduced. He was admitted for vocational training and with proper support, it is presumed that he will be able to complete the training and live a normal and productive life.

12.2 Some people who succeeded despite their learning disabilities

It is difficult to predict the long term outcomes in children with learning disabilities and they depend on the type and severity of the problem, presence of any co-existing problems, age at the time of diagnosis, presence of any other exceptional skill and the degree and quality of support available. However, a lot of people in past and present times have exceptionally succeeded in their chosen fields. These include -

1. **In science and invention -**
- Albert Einstein - physicist, Noble prize winner
- Alexander Graham Bell - inventor
- Michael Faraday - physicist
- Thomas Edison - inventor
- Henry Ford - inventor
- Sir Issac Newton - scientist & mathematician
- Pierre Currie - physicist
- Orville and Wilbur Wright - inventors

2. **In performing arts and music -**
- Abhishek Bachchan - actor
- BomanIrani - actor
- Salma Hayek - actress
- Tom Cruise - actor
- John Lennon - singer, song-writer, actor, activist
- Britney Spears - singer
- Cher - actress, singer
- Nigel Kennedy - violinist

3. **Politics -**
- George Bush - U.S. President

- Winston Churchill – prime minister of England
- John F. Kennedy - U.S. President
- George Washington - U.S. President
- Thomas Jefferson - U.S. President
- Woodrow Wilson - U.S. President
- Anna Eleanor Roosevelt – Daughter of U.S. President Franklin Roosevelt and newspaper editor

4. **Artists –**

- Michelangelo – artist
- Leonardo da Vinci – artist
- Walt Disney – producer, animation artist, theme park pioneer
- Pablo Picasso – artist
- Vincent Van Gogh – artist
- Steven Spielberg - film-maker

5. **Business –**

- Steve Jobs – founder of Apple computers
- Tommy Hilfiger – fashion designer
- William Hewlett – co-founder of Hewlett-Packard
- Craig McCaw – telecommunications visionary
- Thomas J. Watson Jr. – former CEO of IBM
- William Wrigley Jr. – founder of Wrigley's Chewing Gum
- Anthony Parle – MD of Parle Foods

6. **Others –**

- Harvey Cushing – neurosurgeon
- Paul Ehrlich – physician who invented Gram's staining for bacterial study

- Helen Taussig - pediatric cardiologist
- Agatha Christie - author
- Mark Twain - author
- W. B. Yeats - poet
- Muhammad Ali - boxer

So, it can be said that in addition to attempts at correction of limitations, if we identify and acknowledge the abilities, encourage and support out-of-the-box thinking, allocate time to nurture strengths and use alternative ways of acquiring information, the children with learning disabilities can succeed in life as well as in their chosen professions.